Universiteit Antwerpen
Universitaire Instelling Antwerpen U.I.A.
Departement Politieke en Sociale Wetenschappen

Een exploratie in de punk subkultuur

Hans Versluys

Promotor: Prof. dr. G. Kuiper
Verslaggever: Prof. dr. J. Lauwers

Academiejaar 1979-1980

Hans Versluys: London's Burning, An Exploration In Punk Subculture
Political & Social Sciences Department, University of Antwerpen, 1980

2

© Hans Versluys, 1980, 2011 (English translation)
Cover Photograph of Paul Simonon of the Clash (Auckland, 1982) by Jonathan Ganley
Author photograph by Els Tilman
Cover design by Peter McLennan

Written in 1980, translated into English and published in 2011.

ISBN-13: 978-1456435660
ISBN-10: 1456435663

Preface to the 2011 publication

London's Burning: An Exploration in Punk Subculture has never existed in print or electronic format before. Written as a scholarly thesis for a BA degree in sociology in 1980, on a manual typewriter, glued together fanzine-style and illustrated with twice-photocopied photographs (to obtain that harsh black-and-white effect) from magazines, newspapers, books and fanzines. It came with a home-taped audio cassette featuring 30 punk songs. One can still consult the original copy at the Sociology Departmental Library of the University of Antwerpen[1].

For over 30 years, it has only been available through a select number of university libraries, which kindly bought a copy from me at the time. I did distribute a number of copies privately to a wide variety of people in Belgium and the Netherlands in the years after. Its profits paid for my field study trips to Britain.

Over the years, it would get sporadic mentions in other dissertations[2], in online forums[3] and catalogues[4], but actual access to it has always been very difficult. Therefore, I decided to first transcribe the original (Dutch) paper version and then translate it into English.

Many footnotes refer to web sites, which of course did not exist in 1980, but I have added them now for quick and efficient reference.

---

[1] Web: http://www.ua.ac.be/main.aspx?c=*PSW&n=3835
[2] Mark Sprangers: De fonografische subindustrie in Belgie, Katholieke Universiteit Leuven, licentiaatsthesis (1982); Yves Aerden: Tussen Anarchie en Hysterie: De Punkbeweging in Belgie (1976-1981) Katholieke Universiteit Leuven, licentiaatsthesis (2008). [PDF]:
http://static.poppunt.be/attachments/1235389592138/Yves_aerden.pdf
[3] Web: http://boards.straightdope.com/sdmb/archive/index.php/t-115196.html
[4] Web: http://www.ladda.be/html/db_info_detail.cfm?RecordID=219

Hans Versluys: London's Burning, An Exploration in Punk Subculture
Political & Social Sciences Department, University of Antwerpen, 1980

4

There is also an updated literature list because, of course, so much has been written about punk in the past 30 years, and so much better than I did! I would especially recommend Jon Savage's magisterial *England's Dreaming* (1991)[5]. In addition, there are now also countless online resources[6].

In the annexes, you will find a range of blog items written over the years on aspects of punk culture that have retained my interest.

Doing original scholarly research into an obscure and rapidly evolving urban subculture in another city and another country without having access to high-speed transport or communication links was quite a challenge and an expensive one for a poor student since there were no such things as the internet, Eurotunnel or cheap airfares. I did several long study trips, including a Summer School course at the City of London Polytechnic (now London Metropolitan University) with nightly forays into the punk scene.

Re-reading *London's Burning* closely after so many years, I can recall the mood I was in - I was very much in love, despite the at times quite angry rhetoric. It is also quite a strange experience looking at my much younger persona. I shake my head at his dogmatic obsessions and occasional naivety, but marvel at his outright full-on engagement with the subject at hand: at the time, I was a DJ, edited fanzines ("*The Times Have Changed*" and "*Gezaag*") and have organised a few gigs, one of which ended in a full-blown riot[7].

London's Burning is a historical piece set in a time when the story of punk was still very much unfolding and the endgame still a while away – punk's influences are still reverberating through current youth (and adult) culture and art. You cannot read it with the benefit of thirty years of subcultural hindsight. Instead, you have to try to take your mind back to

---

[5] Archive: http://www.ljmu.ac.uk/lea/77472.htm
[6] Web: http://punk77.co.uk/
[7] Blog: http://uroskin.blogspot.com/2005/10/i-had-almost-forgotten-about-it-but-31.html

what it was like living in an exhilarating, if doom-laden, pre-Thatcher era.

Reviewing *London's Burning* now, I would mention three areas that could and should have been included in the analysis, but were mainly ignored due to reasons of space (University rules stated total length was not to exceed 50 pages).

Firstly, the intimate relationship between punk rock and reggae.
At all punk gigs, punk parties and punk nightclubs (Cinderella's Ballroom[8] in Antwerpen was the quintessential example) punk rock and reggae music alternated and complemented each other extremely naturally. Roxy Club DJ and filmmaker Don Letts was the originator in putting both music genres together[9]. You may 'musicologically' speculate about why this is the case - punk rock being an affront to white rock as much as reggae is an affront to black disco - but what was certainly true was that most punks loved reggae too.
And, unforgivably, there is no mention of John Peel[10], who did more than anyone else in promoting new music on the radio, not just in Britain but also around the globe on the BBC World Service, which allowed me to tune in when very few other sources were available audio-wise.

Secondly, the unmentioned proliferation of punk poets.
Punk was not only expressing itself in three- or four-piece rock bands, but by individuals with just a guitar, or who simply used their voice: my favourites were Patrik Fitzgerald[11], John Cooper Clark[12], Attila the Stockbroker[13] and

---

[8] Peter de Koninck & Max Borka: Ooit lag er zeep in Cinderella's lavabo (Uitkrant, 25 Oktober 1985)
[9] Web: http://www.bbc.co.uk/programmes/b0072pzt
[10] Web: http://www.bbc.co.uk/radio1/johnpeel/
[11] Patrik Fitzgerald "*Safety Pin Stuck in My Heart*":
http://www.youtube.com/watch?v=yD8-7QskUS8
[12] Poem list: http://www.cyberspike.com/clarke/poemlist.html
[13] Poems: http://www.attilathestockbroker.com/poems.html

Seething Wells[14]. Not only poets, but also filmmakers such as Derek Jarman[15] and graphic artists (Jamie Reid[16] and Gee Vaucher[17]) went unmentioned too.

Thirdly, how punk enabled sexually 'deviant' young people to feel comfortable to express their queerness.
Although punk had an a-sexual image - or rather, a pansexual one where sex was not necessarily the focus of interest - it was remarkable how attractive punk was for non-conformists in the sexual sphere too. It certainly was not 'cock-rock', and being non-straight was not held against you. I should have argued that punk allowed, enabled and facilitated - but not necessarily encouraged - many young people to come out as gay or lesbian. The opportunity to dress and behave outrageously in order to shock was liberating on a personal level too.

So, with all that in mind, take a leap back in time and enjoy the read.

Afterwards, let me know what you think:
hans_versluys@yahoo.co.nz

---

[14] Official site: http://www.thestevenwells.com/Main.html
[15] Derek Jarman: "Jubilee" (1977) fragment:
http://www.youtube.com/watch?v=7AGbezs1ckg
[16] Official site: http://www.jamiereid.org/about/
[17] Web: http://deepfriedanddoublewide.blogspot.com/2009/06/gee-vaucher.html

Finally, a big thank you to:

Jonathan Ganley[18], for his fine contemporary photos of The Clash, Siouxsie & The Banshees and New Order he kindly allowed me to use as illustrations, including the front page;

Peter McLennan, for the marvellous cover design;

Jacqueline Tweedie, for reading the translated manuscript;

Mark Simpson, for writing the back page note and his advice on publishing;

Ewen Sutherland, for being the all-round good guy and indulging all my whims.

Waiheke Island, New Zealand, 2011

---

[18] Web: http://www.pointthatthing.com/

Hans Versluys: London's Burning, An Exploration in Punk Subculture
Political & Social Sciences Department, University of Antwerpen, 1980

8

Siouxsie Sioux of Siouxsie & The Banshees, Auckland 1983.
Photo © Jonathan Ganley

CONTENT

BLOGS and ESSAYS (2004-2010)

The 31 October 1980 Riot in Wilrijk
The death of Malcolm McLaren
Rough Trade
The death of the single
Punk: Attitude, a documentary by Don Letts
A funny thing happened to me on the road to the Buzzcocks
Generation Knows Nowt
John Peel (1939-2004)
24 Hour Party People

LITERATURE

Books
Papers
Magazine articles

Hans Versluys: London's Burning, An Exploration in Punk Subculture
Political & Social Sciences Department, University of Antwerpen, 1980

11

Introduction

When I decided to take punk as a subject for my thesis, I knew it would not be, in many aspects, an easy task.
As I talked with people about the project, it seemed to them at first sight an interesting subject to study and they usually said they would be looking forward to the result. Often it was for them also an opportunity to ask some questions about the phenomenon. It seemed to me, judging by those questions, that there was either very little known about punk, or that there was an image of punk circulating which was so unreal, exaggerated and unconnected to the reality of my experience. This stimulated me to dig a little deeper to disprove, when necessary, the stereotypes which apparently accompany every subculture.

One source of difficulties was my strong affinity, even identification, with this subculture, which may lead some to suppose I would not be able to keep a distance and be sufficiently critical about it. On the other hand, it was this very engagement and my irritation with "how punk has gone to seed" which encouraged me to tackle the subject.

Furthermore, I am and was afraid I would not succeed in portraying punk culture fully and correctly, because of the limitations of space; the medium of the written word; and my own limited knowledge of all aspects. "Real" punks, people who have helped constructing the movement, may select and emphasise different aspects of the culture and propose other visions and analyses.

This thesis was written in Belgium but deals exclusively with a British phenomenon. The cultural and linguistic distance both helps and hinders the analysis but punk has been traveling far and fast and the concerns, tastes, styles and criticism know no boundaries.

Thirdly, there is the difficulty of the lack of readily available theoretical material about punk. It made this dissertation largely explorative and possibly speculative, instead of the final analysis. You will have to keep this in consideration when reading.

Now a word of thanks to many people, for a diverse set of reasons:

Professor Gerrit Kuiper, who kindly agreed to be promoter;

Professor Jan Lauwers, who wanted to be examiner;

My parents for the all the support over the years and who made it possible for me to study at University level (I was the first in my family to do so);

Patrick Dedrie, for the inspiration and mateship;

Marleen Van Ende, editor of "De Ontgoochelde Frigo" (The Disappointed Fridge) fanzine, for crucial information and sources, and our interesting discussions;

And last, but not least, the "Fan club" Marleen De Buyser, Linda Blockx and Vera.

What is it all about?

Writing a history of a subculture is an enterprise fraught with difficulties. It is nigh impossible to figure out where it started and who, and at which point in time, has kicked off the movement.

Youth cultures have no written creation sources: that was the case with the Teddy Boys, the Mods, the Skinheads, and now too with the punks. As a sociologist in this field, you feel more like an archaeologist: you only find traces of what has concretely manifested itself. You can find apparitions of a culture in clothes, imagery, music, public appearances in the media, societal reactions etc. Furthermore, you could go looking at the social environment, the social, cultural and economic order of society, and all sorts of other things.

[19] Flyer for an X-Ray Spex gig at the Hope & Anchor, London, 1977

Looking at punk up close is searching for points of reference, beacons in the maelstrom of society.

Punks move in the big city and within the city they move in specifically selected places with their symbolically imbued spaces. There they congregate and meet *where the action is*: on the King's Road[20] in Chelsea, the punk boutiques Sex[21]/ Seditionaries and Boy[22], Rough Trade[23] Records shop, the Beaufort Market, pubs and clubs such as The Nashville, The 100 Club[24], The Roxy Club[25] and The Hope & Anchor[26].

After World War II, a new youth music developed in the large cities, rock'n'roll. Punk music is rock: vigorous, loud, fast, simple, energetic, participative and enjoyable but you would be wrong to suppose that punk rock is purely a return to the origins of rock'n'roll without any other content or aspects to it.

Punk rock is mainly a focal point around which punks gather: the music was a means to express themselves, plus a recruitment base for the subculture. This 'new' energetic music and its images attracted especially younger people and this should not be surprising: music was a means to express ill feelings towards a number of social conditions affecting young people such as unemployment, boredom, bad housing, poverty and a desperate outlook for the future.

The appearance of punks mirrored this discontent: clothes, make-up and hairstyles were all symbolic expressions of the

---

[20] Photo: http://cache3.asset-cache.net/xc/94471945.jpg?v=1&c=NewsMaker&k=2&d=77BFBA49EF878921CC 759DF4EBAC47D0AFC8864C3472E86DEA4007C55BC63E4B246265F7E0F31D15

[21] Photo: http://www.unsignedbandpromotion.com/blog-images/matt-early/430-sex.jpg

[22] Photo: http://cache1.asset-cache.net/xc/84144771.jpg?v=1&c=IWSAsset&k=2&d=77BFBA49EF8789215ABF 3343C02EA5486C556A7C8AAC2E725BA815C25F92CBF79410E48074AC4375

[23] Photo: http://i.telegraph.co.uk/telegraph/multimedia/archive/01173/arts-graphics-2006_1173793a.jpg

[24] Official site: http://www.the100club.co.uk/

[25] Web: http://punk77.co.uk/roxyclub77/pages/history.htm

[26] Web: http://www.punk77.co.uk/punkhistory/hope_and_anchor_history.htm

greyness of one's existence and the lack of future prospects. These visual expressions are a thousand times more effective than words could ever be.

Analysing punk culture is then, in essence, an analysis of the symbols and their relationship to an individual's experience of reality. These experiences and their symbolic expressions do not develop in a vacuum. They are essentially linked to other societal actors: the development of punk as a phenomenon is a subtle – and at times brutal and hard - game between youths in a specific situation of repression, alienation, poverty and stratification on the one hand; and the societal border guards such as the media, industry and the political powers on the other hand. On top of that, this interaction is further defined by the structural positions of the social actors within society (as news gatherers, product makers, moral guardians and rule makers) and their linked roles and structural limitations: the discipline of the competitive market; the need for profit accumulation, production growth and publicity; and the necessity to maintain the existing order.

The story of punk is then mainly a story of the battle between these actors: the 'kids' and their frustrations, aspirations, actions and symbols on the one side; and the 'adult society' and its structures and machinations on the other.

Nonetheless, this polarisation is too simplistic: firstly, not all young people turned into punks, and not all newspapers howled in the wolves' choir against the phenomenon. Then there is the social class structure, which sectionally crosses generational boundaries and it is relevant to incorporate that into the analysis: young people worst affected by the economic crisis are those with the lowest levels of education, and they are still found in the working class.
The punk movement will originate in this group of youths, although it is not at all certain whether there is a high correlation between punk and class: a number of punk spokespeople and pioneers have been in higher education.

On the other hand, a large number of underprivileged working class youths think punk is ridiculous and prefer to belong to mainstream youth culture: the careless world of consumption and disco, with its symbols of unlimited success and opportunities.

The interaction between punk (or any other subculture) and society has been responsible too for the development of the punk movement's imagery, ideas and points of view. The sensational reporting of violence at punk gigs by the press is a typical example of what sociologists call a *self-fulfilling prophecy*: after reading detailed and illustrated reports, aggressive types knew where to go.
By wanting to promenade through the world in the most visibly striking way, a look was developed, clothes were designed and poses were struck, which were all greedily reported and exhibited by the media.

Punk is the antithesis of an 'underground' culture: mysterious and hidden activities barely featured because punks wanted to be exhibited as open as possible, spit in the face of authority, and do what they bloody well liked in public, all to ward off boredom.
The media gratefully accepted this openness, and a 'moral panic', which accompanies every subculture, was an essential part of the process.

Then there are the questions at what moment the movement was diverted from its origins, its *roots* and its goals, and when it was incorporated into the mainstream of youth culture and society. Again, this is a complex issue. Just like every previous youth subculture, some of which we will discuss here, punk concentrated on 'culture', which means focusing on a number of symbolic expressions of situations.

Alternatives to the crises in the economy (the dead-end jobs, unemployment, the profit mentality) or in society (living conditions, deprivation and educational underachievement) were only marginally developed: playing in a band, designing your own clothes, editing and publishing a fanzine or establishing and running a record label have only a limited influence. Moreover, they are not as threatening or alternative as they would like to be portrayed. The situation of a large number of young people has not been improved over the past five years; to the contrary, the economic situation and the outlook are not much better.

Punk's answer was too limited to solve its problems effectively. Punk prioritised too much on leisure time activities (if you can call it 'leisure time' when you are unemployed) which was insufficiently threatening to the existing societal power relations that generated its situation.

On the other hand, it is true that the 'punk wave' has helped and stimulated a number of people to realise and express their ideas in the artistic, musical or political spheres.
Today there are numerous bands, fanzines and record labels, which have a massive number of identities, styles and tastes, and they owe their existence and their audience to the punk pioneers. Perhaps Bernie Rhodes, manager of The Clash, got it right when he said[27] *"after the initial wave of explorers everything could finally begin."*

---

[27] In: Muziekkrant Oor (Nederland), 26 July 1978 (my translation)

ETHNOGRAPHY

1. Punk History

There are only just over two years between the first public debut of the Sex Pistols in November 1975 and their split in January 1978. In these two years the punk phenomenon was developed. Perhaps it was this too-short a timeframe which has prohibited the movement to grow up, to mature its ideas, to try things out, to develop defence strategies and to deepen its options, ideology and strategy.

Start and end dates suggested here are quite arbitrary: a youth culture, such as punk, does not spring up on a specific day, but grows in time and circumstance. In order to achieve some sort of historical reconstruction, we can look at a number of salient points when aspects of the subculture crystallised, points in time when things become visible, when the phenomenon 'appears'. The formation of music bands; their gigs; the growth of their fandom; the publication of fanzines; contacts and contracts with record labels; the release of records; articles about punk first in the music press then in general newspapers and magazines; the reaction by the public, politicians, media and industry; the publication of books, articles, films, etc.
We will make a selection.

There is absolutely no doubt that it all happened very quickly.

> *"When it all started off I was amazed. I've never seen any movement move so quick, right, tremendous potential. All the kids caught on to something, they got on to an idea. They had all this energy in them."*[28]

---

[28] Don Letts, Roxy Club DJ

After their first gigs, the number of Sex Pistols' fans grows phenomenally in the Winter of 1976. They can count on their fans to be at every gig and that group even gets a name: The Bromley Contingent[29]. Other bands like The Stranglers also gather a loyal fan base, The Finchley Boys[30]. New bands are formed everywhere, inspired by the examples set by The Sex Pistols, the London SS and The Stranglers, and not only in London, but also in other large cities, such as The Buzzcocks in Manchester. Original fans formed the new bands such as Generation X, Siouxsie & The Banshees and The Clash.

At first, these bands could only play in small clubs because established rock venues were off limits to them. Their fans' appreciation was for the 'energy' and 'honesty' of those on stage rather than 'musical virtuosity'.

31

---

[29] Photo: http://www.raystevenson.co.uk/images/bromleycon.gif
[30] Photo: http://www.punk77.co.uk/graphics/finchleyboys.jpg
[31] Flyer for the 100 Club Punk Festival, London, September 1976

Hans Versluys: London's Burning, An Exploration in Punk Subculture
Political & Social Sciences Department, University of Antwerpen, 1980

20

When interest in these new bands had grown so much in the Summer of 1976, the promoter of the "100 Club" in Oxford Street decided to organise a two-day punk festival in September. A thousand fans turned up together with A&R[32] people from all major record labels. The bands who performed were The Sex Pistols, The Clash, Siouxsie & The Banshees, The Damned, Chris Spedding & The Vibrators, The Stinky Toys, The Subway Sect and The Buzzcocks.

> "The Sex Pistols are the most important group on the scene. They've done what no other bands have dared to do. They've broken the rules, not just the establishment rules but all the rock 'n' roll laws. The Clash are tough, serious and chaotic. [The Damned are a] sheer force on stage. The Buzzcocks are good and honest. Generation X, one of the strongest. Subway Sect are real punks, very simple."
> Mark Perry[33]

Because of a violent incident - a thrown broken beer glass blinded a female fan - punk was banned from the 100 Club and media interest started to happen seriously. A number of special reports had already appeared in the music press[34] but the tabloid and general media started to take notice of the phenomenon now that there were extra-musical aspects linked to it.

The original fans developed their own look[35] to manifest their identity and link to the new bands, an identity that was the complete opposite of that linked to earlier pop music trends such as psychedelic rock or teeny-bob pop.
Hair is worn short and painted in all colour combinations, clothes are black, old, ripped, pinned together and decorated with badges, paperclips and garbage, sexy stockings in broken shoes.

---

[32] Artist & Repertoire, the talent scouting arms of record companies.
[33] Sniffin' Glue, December 1976
[34] An interview with Johnny Rotten in Sounds 24 April 1976; punk specials in Melody Maker 28 July 1976 and 7 August 1976
[35] A fantastic punk home video: http://www.youtube.com/watch?v=x5yoj9m-N1M

This 'extra-terrestrial' look with over-the-top makeup and poses is all the rage in illustrated magazines. This fashion, and 'anti-fashion', was not only created by extravagant boutiques such as Sex / Seditionaries or Boy on the King's Road, but also by the punks themselves[36].
There was room for experimentation, they looked for original styles, tried out unusual clothes combinations, adopted every day useful objects and attached new meanings to them, all in a unified symbols system, to which we will return later.

As mentioned before, record labels started to get interested in the musical aspects of punk.
Stiff Records, one of the first new small independent record labels, released the first 'punk single' *New Rose*[37] by The Damned in October 1976, but the larger companies were quick to snap up their portion of punk bands. Later in October 1976, EMI Records gets The Sex Pistols under contract and releases their first single *Anarchy in the UK*[38]. The record gets into the hit parade and an extensive promotional tour with The Clash is planned.

There is a hitch though: on 1 December 1976, The Sex Pistols are interviewed live on Thames Television[39], and a number of four-letter words are being uttered on air.

The next day The Sex Pistols feature on almost all tabloid front pages and public reaction is huge: almost all venues booked for the tour cancelled their contract, various radio stations banned and boycotted the single and in January 1977 EMI annulled their recording contract.

Punk becomes public enemy #1.

---

[36] Punk home video: http://www.youtube.com/watch?v=_OApKTDPByc
[37] Video: http://www.youtube.com/watch?v=WaOraUh1AyM
[38] The Sex Pistols *"Anarchy in the UK"* lyrics:
http://www.lyricsmode.com/lyrics/s/sex_pistols/anarchy_in_the_uk.html
[39] Video: http://www.youtube.com/watch?v=jRNOUz7uefA

Hans Versluys: London's Burning, An Exploration in Punk Subculture
Political & Social Sciences Department, University of Antwerpen, 1980

22

40

The number of venues where punk bands can gig was decimated, but in December 1976 the Roxy Club[41] opens in Covent Garden and it becomes the Mecca for fans and new bands. Siouxsie & The Banshees, Generation X, Johnny Moped, Wire, X-Ray-Spex, Slaughter & The Dogs, Eater and many others are among a number of new bands who get a chance in front of an in-crowd that is still growing.

Alongside the music, a large number of homemade magazines (fanzines) are being published which sympathetically follow the new bands, report on them and discuss the new releases. The most important and most influential one is Mark Perry's *Sniffin' Glue*[42], started in July 1976. The fanzines develop a style, which influences the development in the musical sphere: news and interviews are disseminated, in which musicians express their vision and ideas; fan photos of their public appearances are published, which give potential new

---

[40] Daily Mirror front page, 2 December 1976
[41] Web:
http://www.guardian.co.uk/music/musicblog/2007/oct/04/roxymusic
[42] Official site: http://www.markperry.freeuk.com/new_page_2.htm

fans an indication on how you too can be one of the in-crowd. *Anarchy in the UK*[43], fanzine of The Sex Pistols, resembles a punk version of *Vogue*.

A number of bands release their first single independently before they link up with a record label with more capital resources (The Buzzcocks' *Spiral Scratch EP*[44] on New Hormones Records, and Eater's *Outside View*[45] on The Label).

buzzcocks

spiral scratch   [46]

Over time, most bands are courted and snapped up by the big record labels: The Clash by CBS, The Jam by Polydor, The Stranglers by United Artists, and Generation X by Chrysalis. Only The Sex Pistols have more difficulty in finding a suitable record company home. The largest companies avoid them because of the past negative publicity – and their public enemy status as the face of punk: they were with A&M for about a week and it was only in May 1977 they signed with Virgin Records. The single released then caused another

---

[43] Front page: http://sangbleu.com/wordpress/wp-content/uploads/2008/11/anarchy-fanzine.thumbnail.jpg
[44] Audio: http://www.youtube.com/watch?v=QoYiQ8Qsozk
[45] Audio: http://www.youtube.com/watch?v=W2quxO36K50
[46] Original picture sleeve for "Spiral Scratch EP" by Buzzcocks, recorded 1976, released 1977

Hans Versluys: London's Burning, An Exploration in Punk Subculture
Political & Social Sciences Department, University of Antwerpen, 1980

24

public scandal: *God Save The Queen*[47] was a (almost lone) dissenting voice during the Queen's Silver Jubilee festivities and the expressions of national unity, pride and greatness. Despite an airtime ban by radio stations and a boycott by several distribution companies the record reaches #2 in the BBC hit parade of Jubilee week.

Meanwhile the first "new wave" LPs had been released: The Clash self-titled *The Clash*, The Jam's *In The City* and The Stranglers' *Rattus Norvegicus IV*.

> *"Punk rock became New Wave when it became an established force [...]. The rather pompous title New Wave indicates a softening of attitudes."*[48]

Almost all bands became part of the pop music production mill of regular, contractually agreed and compulsory delivered vinyl products.

Here and there, some ripples on the moral surface are still visible: The Sex Pistols' debut album is charged in a court case[49] with breaching decency standards because of its title: *Never Mind the Bollocks*.

50

---

[47] Video: http://www.youtube.com/watch?v=TBo0LLlKu5Q
[48] John Tobler: Punk Rock (Phoebus, London, 1977), p 15
[49] http://www.acc.umu.se/~samhain/summerofhate/courtcase.html
[50] Cover of The Sex Pistols' first album "Never Mind the Bollocks, Here's The Sex Pistols" (Virgin Records, 1977)

In the music press, new wave groups become a regular feature and they treat and discuss punk's musical qualities and developments rather than its social dimensions. *Sniffin' Glue* ceases to exist in June 1977 and Mark Perry forms his own band (Alternative TV[51]) to develop his own musical ideas. In January 1978, The Sex Pistols split up during their American tour.

The circle of capturing and new alienation is again closed: the mainstream punk fashion adoption is particularly extravagant, with pseudo-badges, gold safety pins, short haircuts for boys and girls, and colourful make-up. 'Punk happenings' can now be tracked in a number of books and movies[52] about the phenomenon.
Punk records are available in all record shops, new wave singles feature regularly and (more or less) easily alongside other pop genres in hit parades and radio station play lists.
But there are still dissonant sounds audible: the independent labels still exist and are still releasing their idiosyncratic music, avant-garde or primary punk rock, for which the larger labels have no interest (or not yet). There are still bands around, and more join in, who are politically inspired, who release their own records together with long screeds of an ideological or political nature.

Some bands have become superstars, a status they used to despise and a reason why they decided to do something about it. The phenomenon of punk seems to have become integrated and, in the end, defined and accepted as unthreatening. This is only one side of the story because a large pool of talent, in all kinds of field such as music, clothing design, graphic art and literature, was given a fair chance to confront and meet a sympathetic audience.
A taste of anarchy in the UK.

---

[51] Official blog: http://markpatv.blogspot.com/
[52] Don Letts: *"The Punk Rock Movie"* (1977):
http://video.google.com/videoplay?docid=4101813390428941237# and
Wolfgang Buld: *"Punk in London"* (1977):
http://www.youtube.com/watch?v=RYRMXefR-3U

2. Aspects of Punk Culture

2.1. Music

Punk is, primarily, a musical movement: an attempt to bring back rock'n'roll music to street level, to its original simplicity and comprehensibility.

When rock'n'roll and the rhythm'n'blues of the Fifties and Sixties develop into ever longer and ever more complicated orchestrated compositions, punk rock is a reaction against this:

> *"In the 1950s and 1960s kids had a little more to do, access to things. They overtook the music business, the music papers, you had new DJs, pirate stations, Swinging London. That's all gone [...] These kids had to find expression and rock seemed an adequate means. They can't turn around and say The Who's Pete Townshend is great - he's old enough to be their father. [...] Really, the generation of 16 to 18-year-olds haven't had a music which they could call their own. Woodstock's no good to them, not boys and girls going out together under the silvery moon. Their reality is a lot bleaker than that. So it's back to three minute songs, simple melodies, thumping it out. The content is a bit heavier, because it's 1977 and not 1957."*
>
> Malcolm McLaren, manager of The Sex Pistols[53]

Rock music has developed after World War II as youth music. It is a contemporary version of black American blues and white rock'n'roll of the Fifties, adapted to local needs and circumstances[54]. A parallel generational culture developed around nearly every rock variant:

The Teddy Boys of the Fifties were heavily into early rock music made by Elvis Presley, Buddy Holly and Jerry Lee Lewis.

---

[53] Virginia Boston: Shockwave (Plexus, London, 1978), p 6-7
[54] Richard Middleton: Pop Music and The Blues (Gollancz, London, 1972)

This passionate reverence for the old heroes is long lasting. Paul Willis[55] notes fervent fans of this form of rock in the Bike Boy subculture of the late Sixties. Their motivation to 'own' this kind of music is the speedy rhythm, the simple structures and the accessibility of the songs.

In the early Sixties, the Mod appears on the youth culture scene. The rhythm'n'blues variant of rock was adopted as their musical identity calling card in order to clearly distinguish themselves from the Teddy Boys. Speedy rhythm and action are important factors in their music, but the main difference is that they play music themselves, whereas the Teds import their idols from America. The most important Mod bands are The Rolling Stones, The Who and The Small Faces, whose members are all British Mods. When these bands through their commercial success grow into world stars, it is clear that their link with the youth culture they grew from has been cut off.

At the end of the Sixties, the Hippie or Flower Power subculture emerges among middle class youth in the USA. This subculture was an ideological negation of values such as 'success', 'ambition', 'making profit' and a reaction against the 'concrete society' through 'dropping out', drugs, psychedelic rock and rock happenings (festivals in a field). Ironically, it was new technologies, improvements in sound recording and sound reproduction (stereo) and technologies such as 16-track studio facilities, which enabled the Hippies untold opportunities to experiment. The single was replaced by the album (and double album), which allowed restraints such as time limits to be overcome: musicians found the space to express themselves over a longer period.
The psychedelic rock that developed mirrored the Hippie values of maximum personal expression and exploration of your own talents. New forms of musical styles, new musical instruments such as the synthesizer, new designs for album covers and sound effects, in short experimentation outside the traditionally danceable, accessible and simple three-

---

[55] Paul Willis: Profane Culture (Routledge & Kegan Paul, London, 1978)

Hans Versluys: London's Burning, An Exploration in Punk Subculture
Political & Social Sciences Department, University of Antwerpen, 1980

28

minute-song format were de rigueur. The Hippie band live shows too were massively elaborate with light shows and sound effects, where 'personal experience' and the 'expansion of your consciousness' were applied as essential elements of the happenings.

It is easy to see that these musical formats and sideshows are far removed from the daily experience of the working class kid who does not care about intellectualism and rationalisations: the Hippie culture had a very low level of attraction among working class youth. Only in those areas where there was common ground, such as housing problems and the squatters' movement, they sometimes conferred.[56]

As a reaction against the Hippies working class kids would start a new subculture: the Skinheads. This subculture had extra-musical issues they contended with, and we will come back to that later.

In Seventies' pop music a variety of genres is distinguishable. Hit parade music with teenybopper idols such as Mud, The Sweet, The Bay City Rollers, The Osmonds, David Cassidy en David Bowie; American soul music which will transform into disco: Stevie Wonder, Gloria Gaynor, KC & The Sunshine Band etc.; the so-called 'middle of the road' rock such as The Carpenters, Simon & Garfunkel and ABBA[57].

Outside the commercial circuit and hit parades, the Hippie bands continued: Pink Floyd, Yes, Genesis, etc. However, generational working class music in the mid-Seventies did not exist:

> *"[The 70s] was going to go down as one of the most boring decades in history, I should think, musically [...] The Seventies will now be a landmark in history, because of what's gone on and it's all to do with young people."*
> Jordan, punk personality[58]

---

[56] David Robbins & Philip Cohen: Knuckle Sandwich, Growing Up in the Working Class City (Penguin, Harmondsworth, 1978)
[57] Tony Jasper: British Record Charts 1955-1979 (Futura, London, 1979)
[58] Virginia Boston: Shockwave (Plexus, London, 1978), p 5

Most hits were written by a small number of producers for a large number of bands and artists - Chinn & Chapman for The Sweet, Mud and Suzy Quatro are one of the best known. However, there was a generation of youngsters who felt too old for the teeny bop hysteria or the Osmond-mania, and also felt too young, or were too uninterested, to participate in the Hippie era.
Moreover, the earlier idols from the Mod generation were still performing but only in large concert venues where the distance between artist and audience physically expresses the alienation of the rock artist from his roots in the working class youth.

Youth culture and rock music have been integrated from the Fifties: new music and new imagery complement each other. Rock is from this time on a central place of activity for British youth cultures, and for auxiliary activities. The group identity, for example, is a part of youth culture: to form a coherent subcultural group individuals have to come together and develop a distinct set of symbols of communication. Music can thus be the basis for friendship and foster a sense of belonging.

Simon Frith[59] has researched the relation between youth and music. It transpired that young people were most involved with music around age sixteen. They labeled music as a very important means for self-identification and as a source to establish their status among their peer group. Their musical choices separates young people from old, as well as the members of the peer group from outsiders.

> "Music becomes the easiest way for the young to maintain their control of their rooms, clubs and street corners, of their pubs and discos."[60]

Frith argues that music identifies the time and place in possession of the young person, a kind of symbolic area

---

[59] Simon Frith: Sociology of Rock (Constable, London, 1978)
[60] Simon Frith: Sociology of Rock (Constable, London, 1978) p 48

control where outsiders are unwelcome. Music then becomes the context instead of the focus for spare time activities, such as searching for a sexual partner.

However, Murdock criticised Frith's suggestion that age is a better indicator of music use than class background and points to significant differences in listening and reading patterns regarding music media. In addition, he argues that youth cultures get their meaning from their class base rather than from a kind of universal adolescent existence.

> "If all young people have a need for status and autonomy, how these needs are expressed and experienced depends on their different class-cultural backgrounds."[61]

According to him, one should introduce the notion of class into youth sociology and youth cultures. We will return to the relevance of a class analysis in the theory chapter.

Frith himself is critical of interpreting the meaning of music too narrowly: looking at music solely as the symbol of a young person's spare time is not enough. Music is also an activity which is valued and enjoyed by a large number of (also conforming) young people.[62]

As we mentioned earlier punk rock was a reaction the alienation of the popular and psychedelic rock music of the mid-Seventies. We have to look now at how punk rockers tackled this alienation and tried to figure out an alternative.

Firstly, there were the simple, short, energetic songs and from the lyrics and statements of various bands from which we can deduce an engagement which in some cases has a clear underlying political message.

Secondly, there is relation between a band and its audience, which should enable very easy communication between the two. The most direct way to confront an audience is a live gig. All punk bands preferred to play in small venues - mostly out of necessity - or even in the streets or at markets (The

---

[61] Simon Frith: Sociology of Rock (Constable, London, 1978) p 51
[62] Simon Frith: Sociology of Rock (Constable, London, 1978) p 57

Jam started off on Soho Market), partly for ideological reasons. The distance between audience and band was not only shortened, but it also offered the audience a chance to participate in what was happening, to jump on stage to sing along, to dance, to curse and to spit. Song lyrics were about uncomplicated, easy to understand subjects such as unemployment, boredom, authority, media, in short all subjects with which kids could identify and which were relevant to their life's experience.

A band's image and pose were often in complete accordance with those of their audience: band members usually wore the same clothes as their fans, and it happened often that more outrageous clothes were worn offstage than on. After a gig, it is also common to mingle socially among their friends or to talk to those who wanted to get to know them.
The intimacy of a club like The Roxy or other small venues made face-to-face contact easier and the atmosphere congenial. Wild dancing (called 'pogo-ing') and loud sing-along created an atmosphere of unity and identity, a symbolic union of band and punters, a symbolic territory where outsiders were excluded from but interested people were welcomed into.

The boycott of punk from all sides – in the media and by venue owners – forced punk into an 'underground' and an 'outlaw' identity. This 'underdog' label now served to increase the attraction of curious youngsters.
Nevertheless, this forced withdrawal was in contradiction with what punk stood for: acting and reacting.
For Julie Burchill & Tony Parsons[63] many punk band ambitions reached beyond this cult underground status: they were all after recognition in the form of a recording contract. Or in Johnny Rotten's words:

> *"Fuck being a cult, we want to be heard".*

---

[63] Julie Burchill & Tony Parsons: The Boy Looked At Johnny, The Obituary of Rock and Roll (Pluto Press, London, 1978)

Hans Versluys: London's Burning, An Exploration in Punk Subculture
Political & Social Sciences Department, University of Antwerpen, 1980

32

Hooking up with a record label implies an alienation from their original goals, but nonetheless this step was taken by almost every punk band. Making a record means trying to transform the energy and directness of a live gig into the anonymous indirect medium of a vinyl product, mediated by a host of industrial machinations and interfering interests.[64]

The criticism thrown at super bands over their distance from their audience – and thus a proof of their irrelevance – is now leveled by some fans at punk bands (and not only by fans): in music business jargon, it is called 'selling-out'.
The time spent on recording and the associated promotional tours and advertising campaigns have all very little to do with simple 'fun' or with the expression of a social experience in a symbolic way, a way which is relevant to those who it was originally meant for.

On the other hand, a record is a medium, a means to spread rock music and distribute the 'message': anyone with a turntable can hear the music, even though it is always in an indirect and distant way. The contact between band and audience through the medium of a record is not at 'face level', because the message stream is unilateral, while a gig gives the audience the direct opportunity to give feedback on the performance.

Writing the stories of the many, many punk bands[65] formed in 1976 and 1977 is an impossible task. We will have to restrict ourselves to a few examples representative of what was going on. Punk rock bands are spokespeople for their audiences and their ideas. Their statements and actions had an enormous influence on their followers.

---

[64] See Simon Frith: Sociology of Rock (Constable, London, 1978) for an elaboration on the record making process and record label structures.
[65] Web: http://punk77.co.uk/linkpage/punkbands.htm

The Sex Pistols[66]

The media and many punks themselves label The Sex Pistols as the ultimate punk band. They have been the source of inspiration for hundreds of new bands, even though they themselves were not the first punk band to be established (the legendary London SS[67], who never got past a few rehearsals, already existed); nor did they make the first punk record or headlined the first 'punk festival' (those two accolades go to The Damned). However, they had everything going for them: an abundance of energy; a (still) charismatic singer who was elevated to be the uncrowned king of punk, although he detested this label.

> "Johnny has a way of being at once cutting and sarcastic and yet affectionately tender and positive. He'll sit very still, totally inert, his eyes glazed, staring mutely ahead and yet his febrile body, without a trace of indolent flesh gives the impression of perpetual motion. It's as if he's stiffened by an electric current, He's a man of enigmatic contrasts. He assesses character in a flash. To those who come on trying to impress him, he feigns the expected punk façade, revealing nothing of himself. He rarely opens up in public. But to the genuinely curious or friendly he'll be unexpectedly warm. He kneels on the stage and chats to the fans. He smiles and jokes a lot."
>
> Caroline Coon[68]

Their image was shaped, formed and created by Vivienne Westwood[69], girlfriend of band manager Malcolm McLaren[70], owner of a bizarre clothes boutique alternately named Sex, Seditionaries and Clothes For Heroes.

McLaren himself was a genius in dealing with and manipulating sensation and scandals in the media. He knew precisely where the sensitivities lay and how he could cause

---

[66] Official site: http://www.sexpistolsofficial.com/
[67] Web: http://www.punk77.co.uk/groups/london_ss.htm
[68] in: Melody Maker, 19 November 1976
[69] Official website: http://www.viviennewestwood.co.uk
[70] Photo: http://www.thewrap.com/files/u3568/malcolm-mclaren_Sex.jpg

media outrage. McLaren is not your average punk rocker: he is nearing thirty, has studied at university and was closely involved in the May 1968 events in Paris. According to a portrait series in Melody Maker[71], he aligns himself ideologically to international situationism, an anarchist tendency that tries to undermine society using society's own weaknesses and contradictions and to profit from this as much as possible.

If this is the case – and he has been essential to the punk movement's birth, design and development - he has been rather successful in his aims. His clothing designs launched a new image while simultaneously smashing the traditional notions of judging 'beautiful' and 'ugly'.

Furthermore, as the band's manager, he succeeded within three months to extract considerable sums of money from three record companies: from EMI Records around £90,000, from A&M Records around £75,000 and an unknown (to me) amount from the recording contract with Virgin Records[72]. He cleverly manipulated the schizophrenia of the recording industry: on the one hand, their business interests, sales figures and profits with The Sex Pistols as the goose that lays the golden eggs; and on the other, the moral pressure to preserve societal standards in the products that will be marketed.

The Sex Pistols, leading band of the punk wave, also became *enfants terribles* in the media's eyes (e.g. the Thames TV incident). They became the target of bemused people who were shocked by the punk imagery and the perceived threat to society, whether real or imagined: Johnny Rotten and Paul Cook were ambushed in the street, and their records were banned by all media (but they became hits regardless).

---

[71] Michael Watts: The Rise & Fall of Malcolm McLaren (Melody Maker, 16, 23 and 30 June 1979)
[72] Virgin Records PR statement after signing The Sex Pistols:
http://www.rockmine.com/Pistols/SexPR.html

73

The four band members are from modest origins: working class with limited formal education, unemployed or working in dead-end jobs, and they had almost no musical experience – this would become the norm in punk mythology: a preference for amateurism as long as you displayed boundless energy and powers of persuasion. Professionalism, virtuosity and 'arty-ism' were taboo and the traits were identified with the 'boring old hippies'.

> *"I hate solos for two reasons: I can't play solos and I hate them anyway."*
> Steve Jones, guitarist[74]

McLaren may have been motivated by money and politics, but for Johnny Rotten the movement was intended to be more about musical anarchy. He called for more bands like The Sex Pistols because it would make little sense to continue otherwise:

> *"I hate hippies and what they stand for. I hate long hair. I hate pub bands. I want to change it so there are rock bands*

---

[73] Daily Mirror front page, 21 June 1977
[74] in: Sounds, 24 April 1976

like us. [...] I'm against people who just complain about Top Of The Pops and don't do anything. I want people to go out and start something, to see us and start something, or else I'm just wasting my time."
Johnny Rotten[75]

Their song lyrics have a 'political' edge and are not only aimed at shocking the masses, but also to offer ordinary kids the opportunity to recognise themselves in the songs and to sing about their collective daily experiences. What you definitely did not find in the lyrics was the phrase 'I love you'.

"I don't believe in love, it is a myth brought on to sell records, if you try to relate it to something that happens in real life: there's no connection. Love is what you feel for a dog or a pussy. Between humans it's just lust and you end up using somebody for your own selfishness, because you're too weedy to be out on your own. You can get on with somebody real good but do you need to be with them all the time? You get bored with someone after two or three days"
Johnny Rotten[76]

"They're the first band to present teenagers with songs about reality rather than escapism - when there's nothing to escape to. They are facing up reality and through their music they are attempting to make it as much fun as romance was in the past. They believe that the violence of frustration can be channeled into positive action. For all their shocking ability to tell the truth about the world as they see it, they are profoundly optimistic."
Caroline Coon[77]

The loss of integrity is the price of fame: The Sex Pistols became the heroes of their generation, even though not accompanied by massive sales figures as it was with The

---

[75] in: Sounds, 24 April 1976
[76] Caroline Coon: 1988 The New Wave Punk Rock Explosion (Orbach & Chambers, London, 1977) p 59
[77] in: Melody Maker, 19 November 1976

Beatles. Fame came with a number of compromises: performing in large venues, touring (also in the USA) recording contracts and hits. The Sex Pistols became a going concern, in contradiction with their original stance, the link with daily life. In January 1978, the group disbanded.

The Clash[78]

The Clash performing in Auckland, 1982.
Photo © Jonathan Ganley

The Clash is one of the original punk bands started in 1976, answering the call by Johnny Rotten. They too had a very enterprising manager (Bernard Rhodes[79]) – the manager figure in punk looks like he also needs to have a sizable personality – who was a friend of Malcolm McLaren.

The Clash present themselves as a very 'political'[80] group, but they are acutely aware that a rock band can only change little or nothing at all. However, they want to have a go:

---

[78] Official site: http://www.theclash.com/
[79] Official site: http://bernardrhodes.com/
[80] The Clash "*1977*" lyrics:
http://www.musicsonglyrics.com/T/theclashlyrics/theclash1977lyrics.htm

Hans Versluys: London's Burning, An Exploration in Punk Subculture
Political & Social Sciences Department, University of Antwerpen, 1980

38

"I think about who's doing what and what I'm going to do about it, that is what I call politics. [...] The only thing I'm interested in is personal freedom. I just want the right to choose, I don't fancy to be number 528B."
Joe Strummer, singer[81]

The members of The Clash have varied personal backgrounds: Joe Strummer's father is a diplomat and he attended art school. He was unemployed and earned some cash by busking on the street or on the Underground. Mick Jones and Paul Simonon have working class backgrounds but there is usually little information available on punk band members, partly because many of them want to reveal little about their personal lives and pasts.

The Clash became very popular after the 100 Club Punk Festival and their legendary gig at the Institute of Contemporary Art (ICA) Gallery[82] in London in November 1976, but they suffered from anti-punk sentiments in public opinion after alleged violent incidents during their performances. They were also adversely affected by the decimation of the *Anarchy in the UK Tour* where they were booked as The Sex Pistols' support act.

Their debut album was released in April 1977 by CBS Records and was favourably praised by the arbiters of punk taste:

"The Clash album is like a mirror, it shows is the truth. To me it is the most important album ever released."
Mark Perry[83]

Although their music is raw and full of energy, they are positively against violence: their aim is to channel the energy into positive action[84]. Nowadays The Clash is a 'mega-band', good enough for numerous American tours, double albums and different musical directions (including reggae).

---

[81] in: Melody Maker, 26 March 1977
[82] Gig review: http://pages.cs.wisc.edu/~mroman/articles/NME110676.html
[83] Sniffin' Glue 9, May 1977
[84] Virginia Boston: Shockwave (Plexus, London, 1978) p 35

In contrast to The Sex Pistols, who threw in the towel when they were not able to go on anymore, The Clash has continued with relevant, and accessible music and lyrics, however, no longer at 'street level'. They are stars in the pop firmament: the alienation process has worked its way through remorselessly, no matter their protestations.

> *"A song like White Riot[85] is good because it is a classic of its time, but you cannot keep on singing about it forever. They're not on the dole anymore, are they?"*
> Poly Styrene, singer X-Ray-Spex[86]

The Damned[87]

> *"Our music is more aggressive because it's more intense. We like the high energy it's got. I wouldn't be happy in a psychedelic rock band, singing about flowers. I'm not interested in flowers. I'm interested in life today and it's all synthetic."*
> Dave Vanian, singer[88]

> *"Our music comes from inside us and we want to let it out. I suppose as society gets tougher, the music gets tougher too."* Brian James, guitarist[89]

The Damned are not very different from other punk bands except for a number of firsts. They were the top of the bill act at the first punk festival in Mont de Marsant[90] in France in August 1976. They were the first punk band to land a recording contract (with Stiff Records). They were the first to have a hit record with their first punk single, *New Rose*. They had the first punk hit album and they were the first to crash in America.

---

[85] The Clash: *"White Riot"* Lyrics:
http://www.lyricsfreak.com/c/clash/white+riot_20031778.html
[86] in: Muziekkrant Oor, 28 July 1978 (own translation)
[87] Official site: http://www.officialdamned.com/
[88] in: Melody Maker, 6 November 1976
[89] Virginia Boston: Shockwave (Plexus, London, 1978) p 47
[90] Web: http://www.fluctuat.net/4181-Cinq-dates-qui-ont-fait-l-histoire-du-punk

At the end of 1977, the band went rapidly downhill when the fans stayed away because they vegetated too much on their image described as 'pathetic'.

"They became the first lepers of punk."[91]

The Slits[92]

The Slits are a female rock band. It is remarkable that this is not unusual in punk, something that may surprise us because rock music has been traditionally a male domain where women could only occasionally make their mark. This does not mean that all was rosy in the punk period, with female bands readily accepted in the largely chauvinist and sexist world of rock. Nevertheless, we can notice that the number of female bands is reasonably numerous: The Raincoats[93], The Spoilsports, Delta 5[94] and many more. In addition, a number of mixed gender bands with usually a female singer such as Siouxsie & The Banshees[95] and X-Ray-Spex[96].

The Slits have been pioneers. In their appearance, they certainly do not conform to societal norms such as 'ideal types' of femininity: cleanliness, humility, submission, sentimentality, domesticity. On the contrary, The Slits are a flesh-and-blood subversion of this image by deliberately cultivating the notion of 'ugliness' and 'dirtiness', wearing outrageous (or very few) clothes and going on tour with the Clash on their *White Riot Tour* in 1977.

---

[91] Julie Burchill & Tony Parsons: The Boy Looked At Johnny, The Obituary of Rock and Roll (Pluto Press, London, 1978)
[92] Official site: http://www.myspace.com/theslits
[93] Official site: http://www.theraincoats.net/
[94] Web: http://www.allmusic.com/artist/p16950. See also: Adrian Thrills: Delta 5, Rock & Roll Rants & The Personal Dance (New Musical Express, 15 March 1980)
[95] Official site: http://www.vamp.org/Siouxsie/
[96] Official site: http://www.x-rayspex.com/

"She obviously presents a challenge to the very foundations of decency and order - not to mention natural biological law."[97]

They have to fight for their independence and their ideas, and they have to fight a dual enemy: males and females. Against males who do not recognise them as equals and against females who are insufficiently strong in their conviction women can do anything men can[98].

Excitement, fun, boredom, unemployment and social roles are not exclusive to one gender: girls are victims too as well as boys, and why shouldn't they express their situation using 'male' forms and means such as rock music?[99] The Slits defend this ideology by their support in their constructive and creative actions: they play what they want, what they feel and do what they do.

Dozens of punk bands were started; they played, split up, formed new bands, disbanded, disappeared into obscurity and changed their musical sound and genre. Rock and youth culture have a temporary feel and an ephemeral quality.
A few bands remain, just like in earlier subcultures. Others go off into new directions or experiment with new opportunities granted to them by their success. However, always they try to hang on to and relive their original relevance and preserve the energy, which has spawned them. Nevertheless, 'real' punks regard this as dishonest and unreal. Every year new directions and bands pop up, the subcultural scene is in constant flux.

---

[97] Caroline Coon: 1988 The New Wave Punk Rock Explosion (Orbach & Chambers, London, 1977) p 105
[98] The Slits: *"Number One Enemy"* lyrics:
http://www.allthelyrics.com/lyrics/the_slits/number_one_enemy-lyrics-1226503.html
[99] Web: http://www.punk77.co.uk/punkettes/home.htm

> *"The most significant thing about the punk movement is that nothing is definite and the aim is change - any change."*
> Ian Rakoff[100]

Not all the new bands had a uniformity of sound, although many of them did copy each other in their music. Those that have remained successful had their 'own' sound. For example, The Jam[101], at the moment one of the UK's most popular bands, play rhythm'n'blues like the 1960s Mod bands. A group like The Stranglers[102] started with an unusual instrument lineup: the bass guitar was far more pronounced and they also featured an electronic keyboard (and their guitarist is a chemistry graduate).

In 1978, the synthesizer re-appeared - after being dismissed earlier as a hippie and 'trip' instrument - and enabled new avenues for sound experimentation. Some bands even adopted an avant-garde disco sound[103].

---

[100] Virginia Boston: Shockwave (Plexus, London, 1978) p 13
[101] Official site: http://www.thejamfan.net/
[102] Official site: http://www.stranglers.net/
[103] Audio Public Image Ltd. *"Fodderstompf"*:
http://www.youtube.com/watch?v=VczG82Chy-k

Joe Strummer of The Clash, Auckland 1982.
Photo © Jonathan Ganley

2.2   Image

Clothing has a signal function: clothes maketh the man. In every subculture, clothes express group identity.

The Teds had their Edwardian jackets, stovepipe trousers, *duck-arse* haircuts, made popular by Elvis Presley, and *brothel creepers* (pictured).

The Mods were recognisable by their parka coats, shirts, ties and made-to-measure tailored suits (when they could afford them).
The Skinheads adopted a pre-war working class uniform: boots, braces, shirts and millimetered haircuts.
The Punks do nothing else but try to look as strange as possible: anything unnatural, ugly and falling apart can be worn:

> *"The clothes are great and people feel great when they are in them. The clothes have got content, and they are an expression of some kind of comment about the way you feel your situation in society is."*
> Vivienne Westwood[104]

Outlandishness is the norm but copying is often the practice.

---

[104] Isabelle Anscombe: Not Another Punk Book (Aurum, London, 1978) p 58

When punks appear on the street, they deliberately turn themselves into a public spectacle. They invite confrontation by worlds with other clothing symbols and different norms of beauty and style.

Just like all other subcultures, punks claim you have to be more than a clothes-horse when you want to be a real punk. It didn't take the punk ideologues long to decry the fetishisation of the clothes and criticise the hollowing out of their meaning by hangers-on and the fashion industry.

> *"Chuck away the fucking stupid safety-pins, think about people's ideas instead of their clothes. You need more than a few chains and padlocks between yer knees and pins in yer earole to be a Punk. Any fool can spot a poseur. STOP POSING."*
> Mark Perry[105]

What punks hated was the decontextualising of their clothing symbols, ripping off the signs and feelings, which originally suggested and inspired them to adopt the designs into their identity creation.

In an introductory chapter of an overview of British post-war youth cultures, Stuart Hall and Tony Jefferson found that every subculture developed its own style. The 'style' notion means that a number of available good are selected and to which a new meaning is attached and assigned. The meaning attached to goods results from their social use:

> *"Not just things with any meaning, but <u>assigned</u> meaning."*[106]

Style consists of a variety of elements: clothes, music, social rituals and 'argot' (i.e. subcultural jargon).

Punks are no exception to this observation: they selected things that were accessible to them and gave a new meaning to them. We are advised to de-fetishise the objects of a

---

[105] Val Hennessy: In The Gutter (Quartet, London, 1978) p 13
[106] Stuart Hall & Tony Jefferson: Resistance Through Rituals, Youth Subcultures in Post-War Britain (Hutchinson, London, 1977) p 55

subculture, to figure out the symbolic meaning generated by the style and lurking under the surface. Hall and Jefferson[107] recommend developing an *'art of decoding style'*. However, there are no rules to interpret a style uniformly: writing a verbal account of a visual impression is not an easy task, also because it is a subjective activity and its consistency can only be measured against the interpretation of the users of the style. Hence, what follows should be read with caution and the analysis could be interpreted in a variety of ways.

The punk style is remarkable in the use of plastic (trousers, t-shirts, handbags, shoes) and leather (jackets, trousers – if they can afford them). Jeans are missing, and black, gray and white become the dominant colours, symbolising the grayness of the environment they have to live in, the big cities. On the other hand, there are the brightly coloured clothes (such as plastic raincoats) as a parody of the kitsch nature of contemporary fashion. The materials used are simple and especially cheap: old clothes can be bought on second hand goods markets found everywhere in London.

They also found safety pins, chains, pieces of cloth, razor blades and all manner of discarded material, which are not only bargains but also a symbol for the throwaway society, which also throws away her unemployed youth.
You can do a lot with safety pins: 'repair' raggedy clothes, use them as decoration on your clothes or pierce them through your ears, nose or cheek, naturally as a shock-effect because 'normal' society regards it as a useful little tool[108].

Bondage clothes and chains signify a lack of freedom and the coercive submission of the unemployed, poor, young and deprived individual, the *'white negro'*. Walking the streets with your boy- or girlfriend, while holding them on a dog's

---

[107] Stuart Hall & Tony Jefferson: Resistance Through Rituals, Youth Subcultures in Post-War Britain (Hutchinson, London, 1977) p 52
[108] Punk home video: http://www.youtube.com/watch?v=gxoymq-uah0

leash, is a dramatic and extremely direct expression of a subjective experience[109].

Shock and confrontation are the message, a radical expression of a collective conscience of from a future-less underdog position at the bottom of the ladder.

These desperate cries are relentless: social taboos such as sex, pain, mutilation; social criteria such as beautiful versus ugly, male versus female are critiqued in an illustrative manner. The sexual symbolism of black stockings becomes a commentary on the sexual repression by the bourgeois society, which hides away perversities such as sadomasochism or pornography in out the way areas in the city, far away from civilised society. Bondage, rubber and leather clothes bring into the open things of which the bourgeois only can fantasise.

This public exhibitionism causes a public scandal: the newspapers are full of these punk poses. Punk boutique Sex and others become immediate sensations due to their shocking designs: t-shirts covered in porn prose, perverse images[110], defaced pictures of the Queen, naked boys, Christ, gay cowboys[111] and the Swastika symbol[112].

The press is demanding punishment for these outrages.

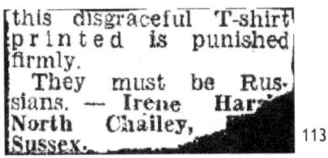

this disgraceful T-shirt printed is punished firmly. They must be Russians. — Irene Har North Chailey, Sussex. 113

---

[109] Photo: http://4.bp.blogspot.com/_uqju_CeBoAc/Sv7X-ZKSzlI/AAAAAAAAAp8/LNasd-pJ0HY/s640/l_7685dc250d8a4444a95ce81f64e3c308.jpg

[110] T-shirt: http://static1.slamxhype.com/wp-content/uploads/2010/08/sedentionaires.jpg

[111] T-shirt: http://ny-image0.etsy.com/il_fullxfull.128912652.jpg

[112] T shirt: http://photos.liveauctioneers.com/houses/kerrytaylorauctions/8418/0165_1_lg.jpg

[113] It also inspired the formation of a post-punk band "They Must Be Russians": http://www.sheffieldvision.com/aboutmis_bands_russians.html

Hans Versluys: London's Burning, An Exploration in Punk Subculture
Political & Social Sciences Department, University of Antwerpen, 1980

48

Concepts such as beautiful/ugly are dismissed by punk fashion as irrelevant: torn t-shirts, second hand clothes, dirty and sprayed in slogans, garbage as decoration. In short, all expressive imagery of punk is an antithesis of the nice, 'beautiful', clean and, foremost, expensive ideal of being 'fashionable'.

Make-up is in universal use and in massive quantities. Here, too, black is the main colour for facial, lips and eye decoration.

Hair gets special attention (as in all subcultures): cut short in many different styles (preferably done at home), rainbow-coloured, as long as it does not look 'natural', slathered in Vaseline gel. It is in fact a comment on the a-sexual image of punk (everybody looks similar and sex is not really that important, in contrast to the hippies) and pan-sexual taste (everybody can look like a sex object).

Wearing black fishnet stockings under a second-hand made-to-measure suit jackets, decorated with safety pins and badges, topped off by a spiked haircut, illustrates the 'female as object' image in society in a crazy and shocking way: a woman is nothing more than 'sexy legs', what exists above is of no importance.
This kind of apparition accurately comments on the sensuality and perversity of an object image: the sexual fantasies in porn literature are being expressed in an extreme fashion on the street: Are we desirable? How sick is your brain if this excites you?[114]

Dozens of clothes boutiques have sprung up selling ready-made punk uniforms. Ripped and printed t-shirts, bondage trousers and leather jackets are mass manufactured. Badges are made by the thousands.

Originality as a norm did not last long:

---

[114] Photo: http://farm3.static.flickr.com/2707/4240543246_ced11ce0d4.jpg

"Today's punks just copy each other [...] but real punk means being an individual. "
Siouxsie Sioux, singer Siouxsie & The Banshees[115]

New recruits of the subculture adopted the old models or wore fashionable punk products. As soon as a manufactured image was designed, it was propagated as the standard punk model: leather jacket, bondage trousers with zips everywhere, safety pin through your ear and green-dyed hair as the stereotypical punk image.

Little remains of the original creative wave. The unpredictable and meandering creativity has had to make way for the intolerant security of a uniform. The punk ideal of constant change and originality appears to have been too difficult. It is, in the end, more difficult to identify yourself with a changing image than with a prescribed pose.

---

[115] Isabelle Anscombe: Not Another Punk Book (Aurum, London, 1978) p 52

Hans Versluys: London's Burning, An Exploration in Punk Subculture
Political & Social Sciences Department, University of Antwerpen, 1980

50

2.3   Fanzines

The third pillar of punk identity is the fanzine, which is a small-scale periodical published irregularly in small editions by punks. They are usually photocopied, home-published, with black and white photos. They are distributed by punks on the street, at markets, in record shops or during gigs. Fanzines try to comment on the scene, interview punk bands, review records and propagate political ideas and theories. Design-wise they use a graffiti-style vocabulary and illustrations.

The punk movement was not the first subculture with its own press. Geoff Mungham and Geoff Pearson[116] report an abundance of fanzines in the Mod era and, of course, the Hippies generated their own literary figures, which commented on and guided the subculture.

Punk fanzines were an alternative source of information for punks, not an expression of the 'official version' of the facts as they could be read in the established press, but aimed to show the other side of the story.
The most important and most influential one was *Sniffin'
Glue*, stapled and glued together by Mark Perry in Deptford, a suburban wasteland in London.

> *"Notice how everyone namedrops Sniffin' Glue and Mark P
> when they decide to write about the new wave. Just shows
> how easy it is to take people in, these days of apathy [...]
> they will fall for any ol'guff!"*[117]

However, he was not the only one. Just like dozens of punk bands were founded in The Sex Pistols' wake, dozens of fanzines were being published all over Britain. Some only ran

---

[116] Geoff Mungham & Geoff Pearson: Working Class Youth Culture (Routledge & Kegan Paul, London, 1977)
[117] Michael Dempsey: The Bible, Compilation of Sniffin' Glue (Big O, London, 1978)

for one edition, others developed into a reasonably professional set up (e.g. *Zig-Zag, In The City*). All are driven by a belief in their music and identity, creativity and energy and motivated to ward off boredom. This dedication to their scene did not prevent the mainstream music press, in one of their regular reviews of fanzines, to critique them for being so slavishly uncritical, for copying each other, for their lack of inventiveness and for no longer being an alternative source.[118]

> *"The useless and often dangerous new cynicism that descended when punk didn't change the universe fell no less heavily on the fanzines, from within and without."*[119]

Sniffin' Glue was the leading voice in presenting alternative visions, interview with new bands and correcting the national press reportage of violence during punk gigs, such as the incident at the 100 Club Punk Festival. Mark P never stopped encouraging his readers to start their own fanzine and in his editorials, he always lashed out at the established music press.

> *"Flood the market with punk writing!"*
> *"Writing about 'punk rock' is the thing to do at the moment [...] Half of them have been to the good ol' college. They've all passed their crappy exams [...] SOUNDS, NME, MELODY MAKER & the new crap ROCKSTAR should stick to writing about the established artists. Leave our music to us, if anything needs to be written, us kids will do it. We don't need any boring old fart to do it for us!"*[120]

Fanzines want to be a readable alternative to the establishment press, whose journalists often have tertiary degrees. Furthermore, they want to draw attention to yet unknown bands, which they find worthwhile supporting and reviewing. The music press now pays a lot of attention to the punk phenomenon by dedicating pages of special coverage.

---

[118] Simon Frith: Sociology of Rock (Constable, London, 1978) p 156
[119] in: New Musical Express, 10 February 1979
[120] Sniffin' Glue 5, November 1976

Hans Versluys: London's Burning, An Exploration in Punk Subculture
Political & Social Sciences Department, University of Antwerpen, 1980

52

Any band, which espouses creativity and originality, is tracked and critiqued by the weekly music magazines – even if the band abhors this attention. That aspect and function has been taken over from the fanzines.

Today many fanzines still exist, and many are still being set up in various fields of interest. Music (*In The City; Live Wire; Premature Burial*) and politics (*Temporary Hoarding*, the fanzine of the Anti Nazi League and the Rock Against Racism collective[121]; *No Future; The International Anthem*[122], by the anarchist group Crass) or a combination of both (*Toxic Graffiti; Kill Your Pet Puppy*)[123].

The whole phenomenon of fanzines looks like a rediscovery of personal possibilities of self-expression, after being frustrated by the established press. It breathes the ethos of the punk movement: we can make our own music, we can write about it ourselves, we can dress how we like and we can amuse ourselves with all that.

124

---

[121] Official site: http://www.socialistunity.com/?p=2102
[122] Official site:
http://www.southern.com/southern/label/CRC/anthem1.html
[123] UK anarcho-punk fanzines database:
http://www.southendpunk.com/html/fanzine4.html
[124] In The City fanzine front page

2.4   Independent record labels

Making a record has a mysterious quality to it: often it is regarded as a privilege and admission ticket to the real rock business, a booking of a place in the rock star firmament available only to a good few. In reality, publishing a fanzine is much easier than making a record, let alone setting up a record label, because records are the result of a complex process that is never under your own complete control. Multi-track studio technology involved in the recording, cutting and pressing the record, promotional avenues and the distribution channels to record shops, all this is owned by a virtual monopoly of large capitalist conglomerates, record companies that have to work under capitalist norms and coercion to increase their profit margins and make a return on their investment. Consequently, only those bands will get a recording contract when they prove to be a sellable proposition[125]. This means, too, that renovation in the music sphere will always come from outside the industry because record companies are inherently conservative and only speculate on current trends, the contemporary pop music which scores hits, i.e. sells well. Anything new is always uncertain and carries a greater degree of risk[126].

At the end of 1976, The Buzzcocks released their *Spiral Scratch EP* on their own label, New Hormones Records[127], an example followed by dozens of others in later years. This was a first step to de-mystify the recording business. In a very pragmatic way, they proved that it was possible with simple and very little means to make and sell a record.
There are even reports[128] of a band, The Desperate Bicycles[129], set up with the particular aim in mind to release a

---

[125] For further commentary: Simon Frith: Sociology of Rock (Constable, London, 1978)
[126] Richard Middleton: Pop Music and The Blues (Gollancz, London, 1972) has a discussion on record label policies
[127] History of New Hormones Records: http://newhormonesinfo.com/
[128] in: New Musical Express, 1 September 1979

record independently. Later on The Buzzcocks and all other big (and not only big) punk bands would be contracted to a record company of a more conventional type, but the seed was sown.

The new small record labels were usually set up in record shops, whose owners were dissatisfied with the mainstream music on offer. Contemporary rock and pop did not agree with their own tastes and they decided to use their available resources and capital to promote new bands and artists they liked but were unable to find a deal with the major labels. Those new artists were either too eccentric or demanded too much control over their artistic output, or simply refused to compromise with big capital.

Again, we must state that this is not a new phenomenon: in the late 1960s, a record shop called Virgin launched a label and these days it is one among the biggest in the business.
Examples from the punk era are Rough Trade in Notting Hill and Small Wonder Records in Walthamstow.
The new labels, which sprang up all over Britain (Good Vibrations[130] in Belfast; Zoo in Liverpool; Fast Products in Edinburgh), have their humble formats, design and ideology in common with fanzines.

A few examples to illustrate:

Rough Trade Records[131]

As we mentioned before, founded in a record shop off Portobello Road and is now one of the largest independent labels. Rough Trade wants to be more than an alternative market stall where one can buy

---

[129] Web:
http://www.derekerdman.com/ilovemilkshakes/october2004/Desperate_Bicycles_Anthology/desperatebicycles.htm
[130] Web: http://www.vinylnet.co.uk/label-discography.asp/label/42/Good-Vibrations-records-discography.html
[131] Official site: http://www.roughtraderecords.com/

obscure singles en albums:

> *"Our aim is to establish a place which would not be a retail outlet where records are treated strictly as a product, but a meeting point where information and ideas can be exchanged."*[132]

Their main policy options are a stringent quality control over all their product releases, Rough Trade owners and employees' own musical tastes and their refusal to sell sexist and racist music.

> *"Rough Trade as a label, as a shop, as a vital meeting place, is a flux of decisions, desires, and designs; a great many notions that intersect, overlap, reinforce, or limit one another on the surface of exchange and aid."*[133]

The walls are plastered with small adverts looking for band members and offering facilities and the shop sells a wide range of fanzines: a vital breeding ground for new ideas.
Rough Trade, echoing *Sniffin' Glue*, does not want to monopolise the output of the movement. They just hope and wish they would not remain the only ones in their endeavours.

Small Wonder Records[134]

It also has its origins as a record shop in a suburbs of London but less ambitious in its aims due to lack of capital resources. It does not offer bands long-term contracts, only one-offs[135].

---

[132] Ian Birch: Rough Trade, the Humane Sell (Melody Maker, 10 February 1979)
[133] Ian Penman: Beat, Activity and Conversation (New Musical Express, 10 February 1979)
[134] Web:
http://recordcollectorsoftheworldunite.com/labels/smallwonder/smallwonder.html
[135] Web: http://www.vinylnet.co.uk/label-discography.asp/label/17/Small-Wonder-records-discography.html

Hans Versluys: London's Burning, An Exploration in Punk Subculture
Political & Social Sciences Department, University of Antwerpen, 1980

56

Small Wonder announced it would stop in 1980 due to its refusal to grow and to link itself to a distributor.

> *"We put our records out because we believe in them regardless of commerciality. I think that's a bit naïve but I don't want to compromise by signing to a major label."*[136]

Fast Product[137]

Fast Product is a one-man-record company in Edinburgh, run by Bob Last. He wants to spend as much time, energy and creativity in the record sleeve design and additional gadgets. Most of his discoveries have found a home with larger record companies[138].

Factory Records[139]

Granada Television journalist Tony Wilson founded Factory Records in 1978 to support local Manchester bands.
According to New Musical Express[140] this the most enigmatic of all the new labels:

> *"They mock and distort the notion of product and presentation [...] What all these people [musicians] do best is playing their instruments and write songs and they should get a wage for this [...] It's quite a thrill, getting things out to people, and it's really very amusing."*

The independent labels appear unable to escape from a number of economic (capitalist) principles: the necessity of growth, capital accumulation and company efficiency to

---

[136] in: New Musical Express, 1 September 1979
[137] Web: http://www.holdingsav.com/fastproduct/fasthistory.htm
[138] Web: http://www.vinylnet.co.uk/label-discography.asp/label/35/Fast-Product-records-discography.html
[139] Web: http://www.vinylnet.co.uk/label-discography.asp/label/4/Factory-records-discography.html
[140] in: New Musical Express, 1 September 1979

prevent losses of resources. This means that a strict quality control needs to be in place regarding their acts. The slightly bigger labels turn into mini-companies, which need to obey a number of economic laws if they wish to survive.

Nevertheless, the political motives of some and the social and musical motives of others have made it clear that there is no longer anything mysterious about recording and releasing a record.

The opportunities, offered to the many new bands on the new labels to elaborate on their musical ideas, have created an enormous flood of creativity: small labels get hundreds of demo tapes in the post.

Furthermore, the minor labels act as prep school for new artists, who, if they are successful in a commercial sense, migrate to one of the major record companies – even if the minor labels disapprove. Trying to hang on to a successful act can cause pressure on its resources and cause imbalances in its cash flow even to the point of bankruptcy. Most minor labels do not mind when their artists tries out with a major label. Small labels also do not have the promotional opportunities or easy access to the record manufacturing plants to enable them to keep a check on the quality of the vinyl used.

On the other hand, the releases by the small labels do get the attention they deserve in the music press.

> "The music has moved [back] into our hands."
> "Less experts, more enthusiasts."
> John Peel[141]

The market monopoly position of the major labels has been chipped away at but not always to their detriment. The small labels, alongside the fanzines, function as useful discoverers of new talent: they not only find new artists, they also try them out commercially first.

---

[141] Paul Morley & Adrian Thrills: Independent Discs (New Musical Express, 1 September 1979)

Hans Versluys: London's Burning, An Exploration in Punk Subculture
Political & Social Sciences Department, University of Antwerpen, 1980

58

The one thing minor labels have undermined is the rock musician's obsession with obtaining a recording contract with a major label. Criteria other than commerciality, such as creative ability, originality and honesty of the artists (summarised as the principles of punk) are applied to give the new talent a chance to shine on vinyl, accessible to everybody to do something with it and to be inspired by.

> "These enthusiastic entrepreneurs, their passion and concern, is a symbol for the whole new R'n'R phenomenon. It is their individual interpretation of the motives and myths of R'n'R that shapes their label and reflects the true feelings of an era. Rock that moves forward, rock that is now [...] The new labels, the groups and the music reflect the speed of turnover, the extent of decentralisation and diversification, the flexibility of the new age. [...] They say something about the times."[142]

---

[142] in: New Musical Express, 1 September 1979

Steve Severin of Siouxsie & The Banshees, performing in Auckland 1983.
Photo © Jonathan Ganley

2.5   Drugs

One of the most feared and panic causing aspects of a number of youth cultures, such as the Mods and the Hippies, is the use of drugs, their addiction and social consequences, such as 'dropping-out', non-consumption and non-productivity, in short the threatening undertone of a subculture expressed in its drug use.

Paul Willis[143] teaches that drugs are selected by each subculture, and only those substances will be adopted which are 'useful' in achieving the subcultural ideal aims. In jargon, drugs are in an integral relationship with their subculture. Willis illustrates this with his participant observation research in a group of Hippies. Transcendence and expansion of your consciousness was a central idea in this subculture, and the drugs that were used were a means to achieve the aim: acid, hash, and heroin - all give the user a floating rush, a trip that takes him to a higher plane of consciousness (whatever that may be). Hippies were bemused middle-class youngsters looking for a world that would make more sense. They were supported ideologically and intellectually by very sophisticated and highly inaccessible theories, philosophies and terminologies, whose understanding necessitates years of study with a guru.

What is relevant for our research is the finding that the adoption of the kind of drug follows both class and subcultural divides: Mods and Punks do not use hippie drugs because they carry the wrong message. They are 'dysfunctional' for their lifestyle based on speed, alertness and action.

> *"There are no drugs in this band."*
> Steve Jones, The Sex Pistols guitarist[144]

---

[143] Paul Willis: Profane Culture (Routledge & Kegan Paul, London, 1978)
[144] in: Sounds 24 April 1976

145

Instead of using stupefying drugs, they use stimulating amphetamines, known as *speed*.

> *"The only drug that makes you sit up and ask questions rather than lie down and lap up answers.[...] It's a useful drug and it's a threatening drug: it raises IQ by an average of 8 points, and it's not addictive [...] Speed has always been an essentially proletarian drug."*[146]

Amphetamines are also in an 'integral relationship' with the Mod and Punk subcultures: they deliver energy and action (a couple of their subcultural ideals) to their users.
The Mods noticed that speed completed their lifestyle, a stimulant that did not keep them from working and earning money, which enabled them to fill their total weekend.

> *"Mods used their drugs instead of letting drugs use them."*[147]

---

[145] Badges, worn on lapels, sleeves, jackets, t-shirts, hats and trousers, were an enormously popular way of expressing an opinion, supporting a cause or band or just to add biting humour condensed on a small disk. They were cheap to design and produce and were as ubiquitous a punk symbol as safety pins.
[146] Julie Burchill & Tony Parsons: The Boy Looked At Johnny, The Obituary of Rock and Roll (Pluto Press, London, 1978) p 77
[147] Julie Burchill & Tony Parsons: The Boy Looked At Johnny, The Obituary of Rock and Roll (Pluto Press, London, 1978) p 78

So, too, the Punks:

> "*Speed is the only drug that can make a prole realise that to make it you don't need more intelligence, just the confidence to flaunt that sharpness in the faces of those who have dismissed you because of your background, the confidence to look down on them. Speed is the only thing that can take the place of elocution lessons.* [Only Johnny Rotten was convicted for speed use and was] *the one who single-handedly instigated the movement.*"[148]

---

[148] Julie Burchill & Tony Parsons: The Boy Looked At Johnny, The Obituary of Rock and Roll (Pluto Press, London, 1978) p 78

2.6   Ideology

The generation of a style, the symbolic use of objects in interaction with your own situation and generational peers[149] and based on the real experience of working class youth as a whole[150], result in a distinctive youth culture. This means that every youth culture has a more or less clearly articulated ideology - an underlying and linking system of ideas and motives – which symbolically links the members of the subculture, supports their actions and gives a 'meaning' to them.

> "[...] registering of group identity, situation and trajectory in a visible style both consolidates the group from a loosely-focused to a tightly-bound entity, and sets the group off, distinctively, from other similar or dissimilar groups. [...] the symbolic use of things to consolidate and express an internal coherence was, in the same moment, a kind of implied opposition to [...] other groups against which its identity was defined."[151]

If the Teddy Boys and the Mods regarded themselves as consciously stylish and modern young people, they also expressed a zeitgeist: the developing welfare state, consumerism and the social mobility ideals of a class-less society. In other words, they lived all these mythologies in their style.

The Hippies presented their actions ('dropping-out', drugs, leading a natural life, harmony, and communes) as a protest and as an alternative to the technocratic, concrete-based society of the 1960s.

---

[149] Generation X: "*Your Generation*" lyrics:
http://www.plyrics.com/lyrics/generationx/yourgeneration.html
[150] Stuart Hall & Tony Jefferson: Resistance Through Rituals, Youth Subcultures in Post-War Britain (Hutchinson, London, 1977) p 52
[151] Stuart Hall & Tony Jefferson: Resistance Through Rituals, Youth Subcultures in Post-War Britain (Hutchinson, London, 1977) p 56-57

The Skinheads were a reflection of the demise of the traditional working-class values and focuses such as chauvinism, sexism and racism, all deeply rooted in the working-class culture but threatened to be rendered extinct by societal changes.

These ideological explanations usually happen afterwards and outsiders mostly do their interpretations and analysis: John Clarke[152] did this for the Skinheads, Dick Hebdige[153] for the Mods, Tony Jefferson[154] for the Teddy Boys, and Theodore Roszak[155] for the Hippies.

This does not mean that subcultural youngsters do not consciously know or live by the underlying ideas. We have seen how important the spokesmen of each subculture are as a source of information: the Mods had their own commentators, the Skinheads the British Movement and the National Front, the Hippies had Rolling Stone, Oz and dozens of 'underground' publications.

As did the punks.

We already mentioned the fanzines, which both reflected and shaped punk ideas. *Anarchy in the UK* published a photo series to create a visual image for punk fans, *Sniffin' Glue* never stopped banging on about starting your own fanzine, and, for example, *Toxic Graffiti* promotes anarchism: do things that you create, think for yourself, alongside a condemnation of violence.

---

[152] John Clarke: Football Hooliganism and the Skinheads (Centre for Contemporary Cultural Studies paper, University of Birmingham, 1973) and John Clarke: The Skinheads and the Study of Youth Culture (Centre for Contemporary Cultural Studies paper, University of Birmingham, 1974)
[153] Dick Hebdige: The Style of the Mods (Centre for Contemporary Cultural Studies paper, University of Birmingham, 1971)
[154] Tony Jefferson: The Teds: a Political Resurrection (Centre for Contemporary Cultural Studies paper, University of Birmingham, 1973)
[155] Theodore Roszak: De opkomst van een tegencultuur (Meulenhoff, Amsterdam, 1976) (translated from: The Making of a Counter Culture, 1968)

The shaping of ideas and the development of a punk profile are also not a purely generational affair. Other social actors label and comment on every subculture, giving it a form and an image not necessarily corresponding with reality, but which can have a negative influence on the further development of the subculture. In punk, the media emphasis on the 'violence' aspect is a salient example and offers an excuse to re-define and re-label other expressions of the subculture, such as behaviour, clothing and music.

If we want to make the punk ideology visible, we have to dig into information sources: subcultural analyses, statement issued by punks, explanations offered by spokespeople, especially band members and fanzine editors.

The Dialectics of Doing Nothing

What does a working class kid do all day when he is unemployed? His leisure activities focus on the street: a football match, a fight, but most of the time the main activity is doing nothing[156], just hanging around, which is a boring experience. Working class youths find a refuge in the street because that is the physical environment least controlled and can compensate for the social control at work, at school and at home. The street and the street corner is psycho-socially regarded as 'our territory' where outsiders such as other youth groups are not welcome and if necessary will be expelled with violence[157].

Doing nothing creates a number of group processes such as talking, laughing, walking around aimlessly, and looking for excitement and weird ideas to stave off the boredom – all these things are generated by doing nothing in a group. Even less legal behaviour, such as smashing windows, youths do not regard as delinquent but being a normal activity as part of doing nothing.

---

[156] Paul Corrigan: Doing Nothing, in: Stuart Hall & Tony Jefferson: Resistance Through Rituals, Youth Sub-Culture in Post-War Britain (Hutchinson, London, 1977) p 103
[157] James Patrick: A Glasgow Gang Observed (Eyre Methuen, London, 1973)

"It emerges from one of the most material experiences of working class youth."
Paul Corrigan[158]

Solving the leisure problem for working youths is a 'limited activity'. Their leisure is socially and time limited: one has to appear fit and sober at work on Monday morning. Furthermore, their leisure activities are economically limited because many, such as going to the pub, to the pictures, to a football match or to a club cost a lot of money. On the other hand they can during adolescence (in work but not 'settled down', i.e. married) obtain a lot on their income levels.

In the mid-1970s, the phenomenon of mass youth unemployment weighs heavily on young lives. When you are unemployed is your leisure time less free and easy than when you are in work. One has to budget severely by cutting down on activities which cost money and by looking for cheaper activities, while at the same time society is promoting a whole raft of goods, services and activities but now completely out of reach. In short, frustration.
This frustration is also fuelled by a sense of superfluousness and of being socially futile: the system continues functioning even though we do not contribute to it by working.

This source of depression does not uniformly lead to revolution, suicide or other panic-causing activities. Punk is but one in a range of options for the unemployed youngster. But being conscious of your social uselessness and lack of future prospects enables us to place the 'nihilistic' tendencies of the punk movement in context: the extreme fashion designs, the adoption of garbage and clichés in clothes and music, the shock element as favourite activity. In short, being the antithesis of the establishment.[159]

---

[158] in: New Society, 5 July 1979
[159] X-Ray-Spex: *"Oh Bondage! Up Yours"* lyrics:
http://www.lyricsfreak.com/x/x-ray+spex/oh+bondage+up+yours_20211257.html

No Future Politics

 Britain experiences in the late 1970s the highest youth unemployment figures since the war. The international economic crisis is a root cause but on top of this, it affects specific segments of the working population. Due to the increasing mechanisation and automatisation in the work processes unskilled labour becomes increasingly redundant. Most affected are young people with limited or no skills. A generation grows up confronted by the fact that they are regarded as complete surplus to requirement in society, in the productive as in the consumptive sectors. Labour-intensive industries are closed down and replaced by capital-intensive companies with a lower wage structure. Instead of offering the opportunity-poor, unemployed young person the chance to be creative and useful, they are relegated to an existence 'on the dole': a doleful repetitive back and forth between home and the job centre, and a complete reliance on welfare[160]. In addition, the future does not look much better.

The consciousness present in a number of very political songs such as Chelsea's *Right to Work*[161] and The Clash's *White Riot*[162] proves that the punk movement was partially politically inspired and motivated. A number of bands are explicit in their politics: The Clash and Crass[163]. The focus points are then: 'think about your situation', 'think about who is doing what to you', 'fight ignorance', 'banish boredom', 'nobody will do anything for you except you'.
Anarchy is the message. However, there is no such thing as a well-defined political programme or manifesto. The punk movement has no ambition to transform itself into a political party. The politics it favours are those of self-action in

---

[160] Weekly incomes listed: £9.70 (Coon, 1977), £7.70 (Frith, 1978)
[161] Chelsea *"Right to Work"* lyrics:
http://www.justsomelyrics.com/432135/Chelsea-Right-To-Work-Lyrics
[162] The Clash *"White Riot"* lyrics:
http://www.plyrics.com/lyrics/clash/whiteriot.html
[163] Web: http://www.punk77.co.uk/groups/crass_in_their_own_words.htm

Hans Versluys: London's Burning, An Exploration in Punk Subculture
Political & Social Sciences Department, University of Antwerpen, 1980

68

solidarity and recovering alienated cultural traits in music and clothes.

We should not dwell too romantically on the spread and internalisation of 'the punk gospel'. Not every young person, who turns himself into a punk or who is attracted to the subculture, always does so with political motives. Some just like certain aspects of the subculture (the music, the image, publishing a music fanzine) and call themselves punks. Moreover, there are obviously quite a lot of youths who have not a clue about the anarchy message: "*Anarchy in the UK? Great fuckin' record. Wot's anarchy?*"
Even setting up a record label has necessarily direct political (undermining) motives. A number of them were started by the eccentric musical taste of the owners.

When punk promoted anarchism, it did so with pragmatic motives. Intellectualism and vapid theorising was avoided. The action focused on small-scale projects: slogans, songs, low-budget activities such as constructing cheap clothes, organising cheap gigs, releasing cheap records and publishing cheap magazines.

Be Yourself and Enjoy It

All punk activity can be summarised as banning boredom. You could dance with wild abandon to punk rock, vent your frustration aggressively, and sweat it all out while having a fantastic time.

> "*Rock'n'roll is supposed to be fun. You remember fun, dontcha? You're supposed to enjoy it.*"
> Johnny Rotten[164]

You can find out from a fanzine what your peers think about everything, what they want to tell you about their and your situation and what they want to do about it. New bands, new records, new looks are propagated and you are being

---

[164] Virginia Boston: Shockwave (Plexus, London, 1978) p 8

encouraged, or even poked, to do something too, no matter what, as long as it is exciting and it staves off boredom.

> *"Every one of you motherfuckers should be a potential H-bomb, not a fucking clothes hanger."*[165]

The 'incredible energy' most punk commentators point to as the most outstanding punk phenomenon is not a fairy tale. At a punk gig, which often only lasts an hour or so, the audience is far more exhausted afterwards than the band members on stage. The time is limited, due to the strict alcohol licencing laws, so everything has to happen at great speed: playing, dancing, drinking, fun, fun, fun: a happy evening out with your friends, excellent, cheap and amusing. Participation and expression are the key words. Do not wait until somebody does it for you. Climb on the stage too. Glue together a fanzine. Be a threat to the current order by showing up the irrelevance of the establishment messages on music, appearance or behaviour.

Anarchy the Theory, Solidarity the Practice

Mungham & Pearson wrote that 'solidarity' within each subculture was an important and intriguing phenomenon in each post-war subculture in British capitalism[166].
Punks are no exception either. Times are hard and resources scarce - they have never been so scarce after the war: the three-day working week, galloping inflation, mass unemployment, regular power cuts - but the social situation and identity is also being translated into a solidarity between peers.
A small example from my personal experience to illustrate:

When you attend a punk gig, British custom dictates you stand in an orderly queue at the venue's entrance. Entry prices are usually kept very low (sometimes free, otherwise 50p or £1).

---

[165] Sniffin' Glue
[166] Geoff Mungham & Geoff Pearson: Working Class Youth Culture (Routledge & Kegan Paul, London, 1977) p 7

Even at these price levels there are young people who cannot afford this. They can do only one thing: beg. They work the queue asking for 10p, and as far as I could see, they got some donation.

You often are stopped in the street by punks begging for 10p for food, the bus fare, or any other excuse. This direct interaction also gives you the opportunity to have a chat.

Both boys and girls beg and it is a custom trait among punks: being poor has no stigma attached, it is a part of the identity, accepted as such and not valued negatively. 'Being poor' is part of the punk image, and as such is cultivated as a way of life, not because of fashion but because of necessity.

Anarchy in the UK?

Concluding the ethnographical part we would like to comment on the questions on how it has all turned out, what happened to punk ideas and ideals and which ones are still around? What has been achieved? What has gone wrong?

Johnny Rotten declared that punk rock was not political but musical anarchy: away from high-mindedness, complicated structures and the big band dictatorships. He demanded more bands like The Sex Pistols, and he got them: the musical activities of hundreds of bands focused on punk rock instead of psychedelic and other genres of rock'n'roll. Punk did not have the commercial impact record labels would have wished for - sales figures and hits were modest compared to, say, disco. The first new wave record at number one in all British hit parades was The Boomtown Rats' *"I don't Like Mondays"*[167] but can you call that punk? What did happen was paving the way for wider musical creativity, expressing yourself with your own means and talent: that musical anarchy has clearly achieved its goals.

The question of whether that is threatening the establishment is a different matter. Many new wave bands do get a large creative and political leeway within the confines of a large

---

[167] Video: http://www.youtube.com/watch?v=AaGnwx62FRU

record label, e.g. The Gang of Four[168], a socially engaged band that has done benefit gigs for the National Abortion Campaign, is under contract to 'The Rolls Royce Brigade' EMI Records.

Flourishing small record labels could pose a possible threat to big record companies. They offer a far wider scope of opportunities for experiment by bands that will not get a chance with a bigger label because of its reliance and necessity for a return on their investment. Smaller labels work with a small budget, which restricts them in their promotional activities. However, they also risk less capital and prefer to work on their label image: quality trumps commerciality and they try to foster goodwill and trust for all records they release. But there are doubts about the 'threat' by independent labels:

> "All this sitting up all night, all this arguing about music, starting little labels, playing little gigs [...] isn't it great to be lost in music, kids? You take it so seriously, it takes so much of your time and mind that you never question or change or stop anything at all."
> Julie Burchill[169]

When a band or artists scores success at a small label, a larger company usually buys them: the contract, the security, the way to fame, they are all the siren call of stardom.
Even the sound has changed. The raw, hard, vigorous punk songs made way for melodious, energetic pop songs, which charted well in the mainstream of pop show business: the hit parade.

There are still punks who are resisting and passionately defend, propagate and apply punk principles. They try to actively avoid being captured by all sides: the record

---

[168] Official site: http://www.gangoffour.co.uk/. See also: Mary Harron: Dialectics Meet Disco (Melody Maker, 26 May 1979)
[169] in: New Musical Express, 12 April 1980

industry, political movements such as *Rock Against Racism*[170] and the fashion industry.

Bands such as Crass, The Poison Girls[171], Honey Bane & The Fatal Microbes[172], Public Image Limited[173], The Slits, The Pop Group[174] and others, each in their own way and often together criticise mainstream society and attempt to be a living proof that alternatives can exist and work.

These bands do not limit themselves to music. They value their message and quality. They not only produce music but also accompany their work with all sorts of visual additions such as foldout posters, pamphlets and interviews.

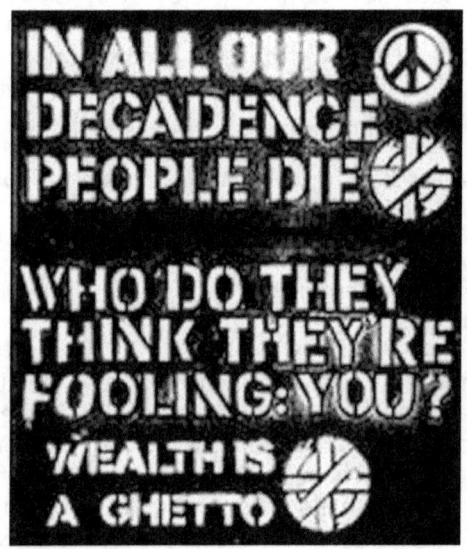

175

[170] Official site: http://www.rockagainstracism.org/. See also: Angus MacKinnon & Charles Shaar Murray: RAR, It's Number One, It's Top of the Agitpops (New Musical Express, 24 March 1979) and Steve Clarke: Masterminding the Militant Roadshow (New Musical Express, 31 March 1979)
[171] Official site: http://www.poisongirls.co.uk/
[172] Web: http://www.last.fm/music/Fatal+Microbes
[173] Official site: http://www.pilofficial.com/info.html
[174] Simon Frith: Afterpunk, The Different Drummer (Melody Maker, 31 March 1979)
[175] Crass poster, lyrics from "*Shaved Women*":
http://www.mp3lyrics.org/c/crass/shaved/

All adhere to an anarchist creed, mixed with feminism and anti-racism, but also anti-political (mainly aimed against the National Front and the Socialist Workers' Party). Like clockwork, they send messages into the world and they have a hardcore following.

Crass is a very popular band and they try to keep punk ideals alive ('think for yourself', 'do something', 'anarchy, peace and freedom') and to transmit them.

The main point is to try to offer a political alternative, which transcends the area of leisure, to work out the practicalities of and the propagation of anarchism. Crass, The Poison Girls and Honey Bane live together on a farm in Epping, Essex. They organise their own activities and, of course, they meet difficulties in trying to arrange gigs. When they want to do benefit gigs, they meet resistance from all sides: due to their appearance and their political convictions, they are not appreciated by the left or the right and, to the contrary, are actively boycotted. The violent eruption during a Crass-gig in Conway Hall, London in September 1979[176] was caused by Socialist Workers Party, Rock Against Racism and Anti-Nazi League militants who fought National Front adherents. Afterwards all blame was laid on Crass due to their 'insufficient selection and vetting' of their audience members.[177]

Those analyses are, in my opinion, too narrow in their scope: the finger is pointed at "THE SYSTEM", the anonymous, irreducible bad man, the cause of all trouble, social problems, war and misery. The theoretical explanations remain vague or are even non-existent: paranoia?

Desperation and misery battled by consciousness-raising alienation.

---

[176] Web:
http://i208.photobucket.com/albums/bb227/killyourpetpuppy/Print%20mate
rial/ConwayHallThelevellerOct79.jpg
[177] Refer for further discussion: Toxic Graffiti, Late 1979

Hans Versluys: London's Burning, An Exploration in Punk Subculture
Political & Social Sciences Department, University of Antwerpen, 1980

74

The future starts here.

New Order, performing in Auckland 1982.
Photo © Jonathan Ganley

THEORY

In this part, we will attempt to analyse the punk phenomenon in a sociological and theoretical frame.

Punk as a youth subculture is embedded in a social structure together with, and opposite to, the working class community on the one hand and the dominant culture of the establishment on the other hand.

In order to understand the origins of youth cultures, we have to look at social changes and their mythological status in post-war society. Then we will be able to look more closely at working class youth subcultures, their points, aim, analyses and weaknesses. Their 'failure' gets special attention: they appeared and disappeared again. What was their influence on 'improving' the subcultural young person's situation? What solutions and answers did the subcultures have on offer? What social reactions did they cause and how can they be analysed? In conclusion, we will look at the range of problems each youth subculture faces in realising its aims.

3.1   Culture, Subculture and Working Class Youth Culture: Positional Schema and Definitions

If we want to discuss culture, subculture and working-class youth culture, we cannot do without a couple of definitions first.
The level on which social groups develop different patterns in their way of life and give expression to their social and material experience of life we want to collate under the term 'culture'.

> *"The culture of a group or a class is the peculiar and distinctive 'way of life' of the group or class, the meanings, values and ideas embodied in institutions, in social relations, in systems of beliefs, in mores and customs, in the uses of objects and material life."*[178]

Culture is a set of acts, a practice by people who by living together give sense to their community.

This culture is a 'guide of meanings' which is not only internalised in the minds of individuals, but is also objectified in institutions and social patterns of organisation which socialise the individual. Culture gives form to social relationships and is the way in which these relationships are experienced and interpreted. Every individual is born into a matrix of relationships, institutions and meanings, which enable him access and localisation within a 'culture'. Human beings create their own culture but they are limited by their structural positions within a class, within the production system and within society as a whole:

> *"Men make their own history but they do not make just as they please; they don't make it under circumstances*

---

[178] Stuart Hall & Tony Jefferson: Resistance Through Rituals, Youth Subcultures in Post-War Britain (Hutchinson, London, 1977) p 10

> *chosen by themselves, but under circumstances directly encountered, given and transmitted from the past.*"
> Karl Marx[179]

Every group in society will develop its own culture. In addition, every group knows about other group cultures. However, just as groups have unequal power in society, their culture will also differ in strength. The 'definitions of the world' will be a function of this cultural power. The group, which has the most influence, power and weight, will propagate its definition of the world as the 'legitimate' one, according to Gramsci's theory of cultural hegemony[180].
The cultures of other social groups are not only be subordinate to the hegemonic, dominant culture, but will also fight this hegemony, just like there is a struggle over social and economic topics.

We should not limit ourselves to developing a simplistic scheme. Within each culture, there is no uniformity: the hegemonic culture comprises of a range of factions such as the aristocracy, the merchant bourgeoisie and the clergy, which do not always see eye to eye on ethics or ideology. Within the subordinate classes a similar variety of battle lines between middle class, working class, races and ages. 'Cultural class warfare' is not always manifest as periods of relative calm and co-existence alternate with turbulent times.

The simplistic term 'culture' is too abstract to label real historical events in society more accurately than simply describing them. The term needs to be opened up to the group it belongs to.
The most fundamental groupings in society are social classes and the most fundamental cultures are class cultures[181].

---

[179] Quoted by Stuart Hall & Tony Jefferson: Resistance Through Rituals, Youth Subcultures in Post-War Britain (Hutchinson, London, 1977) p 10
[180] Bob Lumley: Gramsci's Writing on the State and Hegemony (Centre for Contemporary Cultural Studies paper, University of Birmingham, 1977)
[181] Stuart Hall & Tony Jefferson: Resistance Through Rituals, Youth Subcultures in Post-War Britain (Hutchinson, London, 1977) p 6

These class cultures are big networks comprising smaller, localised and structured entities, the subcultures.

A youth culture is one such subculture within the bigger framework of a parent culture. Essentially this means the subjects that are of interest to a youth culture derive from the parent culture, and they have many concerns in common. Due to its unique position, a separate culture will develop in relation to its situation. In order to develop an identity separate from the parent culture, a separate sphere of interests will be focused on their own activities, the use of materials, meeting places etc.

A separate working class youth culture has a double link up, both with the parent culture - the working class culture from which it is relatively autonomous – and with the dominant culture, which it is submissive to.

The term 'youth culture' signifies a group of young people who congregate around specific activities, topics and in defined territories. When looking at these youth cultures we must take those double links with the working class culture and the dominant culture into consideration.

3.2   Youth, Youth Culture and Subculture: the Ideology of Classlessness

However, the terms 'youth' and 'youth culture' are not useful either for analytical purposes, according to Hall and Jefferson, and Frith. Those terms are too simple and only describe reality. Youth is an "ideologically loaded concept"[182] because it obscures the class boundaries and suggests classlessness, or in other words, it suggests a break in the old class boundaries and the formation of new 'classes' or 'social categories' defined by new criteria such as age.

There are many reasons why class analysis was abandoned after the war[183]. The Cold War is one: it discouraged every class analysis. Attention in youth research focused on the young person's 'own world' decoupled from the adult world[184]. The increase in incomes and the arrival of the welfare state in general, the promotion of the image of a 'teenager', the carefree, universal, young consumer in the media, portraying youth as a homogenous group of consumers with uniform needs and aspirations is a second factor. Increases in a teenager's budget have created a separate teenage market place, and simultaneously the opportunity to spread a uniform image of youth. The rise of the mass media contributes to the possibilities of imitation and manipulation on a grand scale. Images are being distributed everywhere. Who of us would have heard of punks if they had not appeared in every illustrated magazine or newspaper?

The society of abundance and wellbeing seems to have erased class differences. Youth culture is turned into a pure market phenomenon and one element in the exploitation of youth.

---

[182] Simon Frith: Sociology of Rock (Constable, London, 1978) p 23
[183] Geoff Mungham & Geoff Pearson: Working Class Youth Culture (Routledge & Kegan Paul, London, 1977) p 13
[184] James Coleman: The Adolescent Society (The Free Press, Glencoe, Il, 1961)

Youth and youth culture are nonetheless of recent vintage. There are sporadic indications of a something resembling youth culture before the war[185], but both youth and youth culture are both post-war phenomena. There are various reasons for this:

One, in the rise of the new welfare state all sections of society partook in the increase in standards of living, although not equitably. Youth incomes rose a great deal[186]: the economic basis, i.e. the ability to be an independent consumer, was sustained by this financial autonomy.

Two, the rise of mass media and mass culture, mentioned before.

The third reason is emotional, but nonetheless socially relevant: the war and the atom bomb. Children born during or after the war live more or less constantly conscious of a violent social context. Hall & Jefferson point to explanations of the violence by the Teddy Boys using that element. War and violence play a part in every subculture: the actions and self-assuredness of the Mods, the pride and chauvinism of the Skinheads, the love and peace ideas of the Hippies and the 'no future' idea of the Punks.

Four, the extension of compulsory education, the opportunity to get an education independent of your means and origins, and longer education in general cause an extension in time between childhood and adulthood. Adolescence creates its own conditions and its own in-group interactions outside adult society.

The last developments are in new styles and forms of music: a unique image, its own musical genre and a unique scene. Elvis

---

[185] Stuart Hall & Tony Jefferson: Resistance Through Rituals, Youth Subcultures in Post-War Britain (Hutchinson, London, 1977) p 17
[186] Mark Abrams: Teenage Consumer Spending in 1959 (London Press Exchange, 1961)

Presley, The Beatles, Pink Floyd and The Sex Pistols are all 'rallying points' of a spontaneous and commercial community. There is nevertheless an ideological, i.e. masking, aspect to the image of the welfare state:

Abundance

The higher participation of the lower social classes in the rising wealth is irrefutable, but this is relative as differences between the rich and the less wealthy remain, and so did a clear group of poor people[187]. These differences become significant in times of economic recession as in the 1970s. The unskilled and low skilled were hit first and hardest. The consequences of the recession are not equally shared between social classes.

Consensus

A degree of general political consensus between the major political parties can be noticed when the British Labour Party abandoned a 'real' socialist manifesto and adopted a social-democrat image, aimed at humanising hard capitalism using a reformist policy. Election campaigns after the war always concentrate on the middle of the political spectrum, the floating voters, who may be put off by policies considered too radical (or attracted by a populist anti-Labour ones like in 1979). This led to diminishing fundamental differences between the two main parties' policy platforms. Fact is that working class people do not hesitate to swing their vote between Labour and Conservative. This supposed political consensus is still very much a mirage. Immigration, Government intervention and income redistribution policies are still major points of difference. In addition, we should not forget union militancy.

---

[187] Herman Deleeck: Ongelijkheden in de welvaartstaat (De Nederlandsche Boekhandel, Antwerpen, 1977)

Embourgeoisement

This term emerges from an amalgamation of the previous terms of economic abundance and political consensus. It suggests a capturing, an assimilation of the working class into a middle class way of life. Various causes can be picked out: the removal of old run down neighbourhoods, the construction of new housing in the outer suburbs, television, the automobile, the creature comforts at home[188] and the democratisation of education.

Nevertheless, this bourgeoisification of the working class still raises questions. Abundant research into educational participation of the lower classes found ample evidence that class differentiation in educational establishments has not disappeared[189]. Nor has union militancy gone away, as evidenced empirically by the strikes during the 'Winter of Discontent' in previous years.

If we look critically at society as a whole, we must be even more critical when looking at its youth. A legendary study[190] of the teenage consumer found a separate, autonomous teenage market, but a closer look revealed that it only referred to working class youngsters. Working class kids leave school earlier than their middle class peers do. However, due to a time lag before they settle down, there is a period in the life of the adolescent providing him with a relatively high income which does not have to be spent on life's necessities but instead in the leisure sphere.

There is no uniformity within this group of working young people. There are skilled and unskilled, males and females[191],

---

[188] Michael Young & Peter Wilmott: Family and Kinship in East London (Routledge & Kegan Paul, London, 1969)
[189] Guido De Corte, Universiteit Antwerpen, Department Didaktiek en Kritiek, lecture notes, 1980
[190] Mark Abrams: Teenage Consumer Spending in 1959 (London Press Exchange, 1961)
[191] For girls in subcultures, see: Angela McRobbie & Jenny Garber, in: Stuart Hall & Tony Jefferson: Resistance Through Rituals, Youth Subcultures in Post-War Britain (Hutchinson, London, 1977) p 209-222

each with their own possibilities and ambitions. Not only is there a difference in financial rewards between those groups, they also differ in, for example, job mobility. Unskilled workers change jobs more frequently than skilled ones and Simon Frith even suggests[192] a difference in work dedication due to a more career-oriented motivation and value their job security more but he adds this is not a scientific certainty. In the 1960s and 1970s, the student market becomes also relevant, especially for rock music.

'Youth' consists of various factions, classes, each in their own material situation and with their limitations and possibilities. When looking at the various youth cultures that have developed among 'youth', we should also consider the class and structural positions and backgrounds. Subcultures are but one answer to the problems that confront young people. These problems are not just confronting youth, because the social situation in which these problems arise also affect the parent culture, which includes young people, as we have mentioned before. The development of a subculture should be seen in terms of the implications of membership of a broader, subordinate parent culture[193].

An analysis of youth culture will need to contain a class analysis too. Phil Cohen has developed a sophisticated youth culture theory[194]. According to him, youth cultures express the latent contradictions inside the parent culture. These contradictions have a broad social basis and origins as social changes after the war destroyed traditional neighbourhoods and a working class way of life. The main factors of change were the re-housing in high-rise estates, the fragmentation of extended family kinships into nuclear families, and industrial changes such as labour restructuring, automatisation and the diminishing share of labour in the production process. These

---

[192] Simon Frith: Sociology of Rock (Constable, London, 1978) p 33
[193] Stuart Hall & Tony Jefferson: Resistance Through Rituals, Youth Subcultures in Post-War Britain (Hutchinson, London, 1977) p 29
[194] Phil Cohen: Subcultural Conflict and Working Class Community (Centre for Contemporary Cultural Studies paper, University of Birmingham, 1972)

social changes had a direct impact on the working class culture of a 'neighbourhood', which is a central concept in working class culture. The neighbourhood has always been the basis of class solidarity and has nourished the cultural identity of the working class in the UK[195].

These social changes undermined this solidarity and culture. The neighbourhood disappeared; the supermarket, the local park and the inner city leisure facilities, all far removed from home, replaced communal spaces, such as the corner shop, the pub and the street corner. Cohen argues there were only two directions open to East Enders (the subject of his research): the 'upward-mobile elite worker' and those left behind "downward into lumpen".

The important thing here is seeing how social and economic changes have torpedoed any defence mechanisms of the working class culture. It thus also nuances the *embourgeoisement* concept: the working class did not disappear into the middle class but was broken up into several options, each going their own way and rooted in their own social and economic circumstances.

The main point of Cohen's theory is that social changes have impacted both on parents as on young people in the East End but the 'answers' of the generations differed according to age and positions in the life cycle, experiences and material conditions. Young people felt these changes in a very direct way. Paid work became more and more available outside the local community – or disappeared altogether. The latent function of subcultures, which sprang up, was an 'ideological solution' to the problem. A solution not rooted in reality but in an 'imaginary' way:

> *"Mods, Parkers, Skinheads and Crombies are a succession of subcultures which all correspond to the same parent culture and which attempt to work out through a series of*

---

[195] Michael Young & Peter Wilmott: Family and Kinship in East London (Routledge & Kegan Paul, London, 1969)

*transformations, the basic problematic, or contradictions,
which is inserted in the subculture by the parent-culture.
So you can distinguish three levels in the analysis of
subcultures: one is the historical, which isolates the
specific problematic or a particular class fraction;
secondly, the subsystems and the actual transformations
they undergo from one subcultural moment to another;
thirdly, the way the subculture is lived out by those who
are its bearers and supporters.* "[196]

Hall and Jefferson's criticism[197] of this approach open up the
theory a bit wider: why do the Mods explore into the
upwardly mobile direction and the Skinheads into the
downward one? The relation with and the influence of the
contradictions in the parent culture on youth and their
crystallisation into a subculture is complex and subtle.

Developing solutions in an ideological manner and living in
relation to your material conditions in an 'imaginary' way is
not restricted to people who join subcultures. Others do that
too. They suggest that these sorts of analyses emphasise too
much the 'reading' of subcultures and too little on the
material, economic and social position of the subcultural
'solution'.

---

[196] Phil Cohen: Subcultural Conflict and Working Class Community (Centre for
Contemporary Cultural Studies paper, University of Birmingham 1972)
[197] Stuart Hall & Tony Jefferson: Resistance Through Rituals, Youth
Subcultures in Post-War Britain (Hutchinson, London, 1977) p 33

Hans Versluys: London's Burning, An Exploration in Punk Subculture
Political & Social Sciences Department, University of Antwerpen, 1980

86

3.3 An Overview of Subcultural Responses by Working Class Youth Cultures

The development of a subculture is one of the possible responses by the working class youth to their situation and is the expression of the latent but mediated contradictions within the parent culture. Nonetheless, we must not forget the complex relationship that youth cultures have with other social actors: their peers; adult strategies and reactions; other subcultures and, last but not least, the dominant culture and its control instruments.

The development of a subculture is always a subtle game between all these actors and we will illustrate them below.

The subcultural answers are not always of the ideological kind but also rooted in reality: gaining space and autonomy from the authorities in charge, the symbolism of the street corner, the pub, the rehearsal basement, the disco or a piece of urban wasteland.

The Teddy Boys[198]

In his study[199] of Teds, Tony Jefferson explains how a number of post-war changes and developments have stimulated, or even caused the Teddy Boy culture.

The first social change was 'ecological': the destruction of the slums and, simultaneously, the aforementioned neighbourhood culture, the re-housing and the disappearance of communal spaces and solidarity. Immigrants move into the abandoned areas and instantly change the character of the neighbourhood.

---

[198] Photo:
http://www.jukeboxbritain.co.uk/ch%205%20Teddy%20Boys%20(2).jpg
[199] Tony Jefferson: The Teds: a Political Resurrection (Centre for Contemporary Cultural Studies paper, University of Birmingham, 1973)

A second social change was in the educational area: the Education Act (1944) opened up all schools to anyone with sufficient academic capabilities. The aim was to introduce classlessness into general education. Jefferson argues that the social effects of the Act deteriorated the position of the early school leaver. Failing at school was now socially regarded as a 'personal failure' because it could no longer be blamed on the school selection criteria. According to Jefferson, the media also spread this myth of the openness of education.

In the political sphere, the post-war period is characterised by an increasing 'political consensus': priorities were the construction of the welfare state, the mixed economy and the humanization of capitalism. The traditional schism between Conservative and Labour is being undermined at the same time as the traditional gap between 'us' and 'them' in the political convictions of the working class. Labour Party changes in policies and convictions that do not differ that much any more from the traditional political right, helped too.

In the economic sphere, we see the birth of the society of affluence. This euphoria and era of full employment cause extra isolation of those who are without work: the Teds were the main unemployed group because compulsory military training was still a feature in their life and employers were not keen on hiring those that faced conscription. The Education Act also made the link between training and future jobs stronger, while deteriorating the prospects for the low and unskilled. Jefferson argues that due to those structural inequalities and the discrimination in the social and economic spheres, Teddy Boy life crucially focuses on leisure time.

> *"It was the area where grievances engendered in other areas were felt most – where the contradictions endemic in*

> *other areas in their lives were worked out and [...]*
> *'magically' resolved.* [200]

In the 1950s, leisure facilities were not widespread yet and still undeveloped. So what was the Teddy Boy answer?

> *"An attempt to defend, symbolically, a constantly threatened space and a declining status.* [201]

The subcultural grouping is seen as a replacement of the traditional extended family and its solidarity functions. The territorial feelings of the Teds are linked to this. Moreover, Teddy Boys were extremely sensitive to perceived insulting remarks regarding their persons, group or appearance. This is because these insults rob them of the little status and space they have. The violence in their fights could be seen in this light too. The attacks on, for instance, Cypriot café owners and black immigrants can be interpreted as a defence of their status. The Teds rationalised their own bad social situation as a consequence of the contemporary waves of immigration. They channeled their frustration into violence against those social groups they regarded as economically successful.

Nine unskilled working class adolescents were severely punished by the authorities for causing the race riots of 1958[202].

> *"The scape-goating involved is a sure sign of mystification at work - the protective cloak of the ruling classes being drawn closer to prevent its real interests becoming too visible.* [203]

---

[200] Tony Jefferson: The Teds: a Political Resurrection (Centre for Contemporary Cultural Studies paper, University of Birmingham, 1973) p 6
[201] Tony Jefferson: The Teds: a Political Resurrection (Centre for Contemporary Cultural Studies paper, University of Birmingham, 1973) p 7
[202] Web:
http://www.20thcenturylondon.org.uk/server.php?show=conInformationReco rd.161
[203] Tony Jefferson: The Teds: a Political Resurrection (Centre for Contemporary Cultural Studies paper, University of Birmingham, 1973) p 8

The Mods[204]

The Mods were champions in working out the notion of 'style'. When looking at their way of life it is necessary to consider the social and economic background. At the start of the Mod period, in the early 1960s, the UK experienced a further expansion of the welfare state. Wages kept on rising, the number of consumer goods on sale increased massively and post-war rationing was a thing of the past.

Mods were working class youngsters who lived a perfect imaginary life contrasted to their real situation. They were the hard expression of the myth of the upwardly mobile worker. Although they had low value jobs, in their spare time you could not distinguish them from a middle class white-collar worker. Just like the Teds, their leisure time focused on a number of topics: clothes, music, scooters and speed.
This focus on consumption, nevertheless, could lead to the wrong conclusion that Mods were purely a construct of the fashion and music industries:

> "The mod was never a passive consumer, as his hedonistic middle class descendent [the hippie] often was."[205]

The Mods commented on the society of consumption because they adopted a lifestyle mirroring the ultimate 1960s person: the classless, careless and stylish consumer.

In the media, Mod life was portrayed as sensational, full of action and glamour, and the Mods tried to live out this image (a good illustrative example is the movie *Quadrophenia*[206]). Their real lives were far less glamorous: dead end jobs, poor housing and an obsession, consequently, for their leisure time dominated their lives. During their non-working time, they grabbed the chance to up their status by working out a style

---

[204] Photo: http://www.retrowow.co.uk/retro_style/60s/mods.gif
[205] Dick Hebdige: The Style of the Mods (Centre for Contemporary Cultural Studies paper, University of Birmingham, 1973) p 8
[206] Photo: http://www.westenders.org/67_quadrophenia.jpg

emphasized by a number of highly valued middle class characteristics such as appearance and consumption.

> *"The importance of style to the Mods can never be overstressed - Mod was pure, unadulterated STYLE - the essence of style."*[207]

Their style could be read against this background: the scooter as a respectable mode of transport (in contrast to having to catch the working class bus), clothes as a communication medium (signal and identity) and as a symbol of solidarity. Speed pills gave them the opportunity to use their leisure time as productive as possible and to prevent them from 'bad' behaviour such as being lazy and sleeping.

> *"It was like taking over the country"* (on the beachfront riots in Margate in 1964)[208]

In Cohen's theory we have seen that he labeled the Mods as the working class youth faction which took the 'upward' option and they were an expression of the ideological contradiction within the working class parent culture (the *embourgeoisement* trend). The Mods would take over this bourgeois role and its way of life to express their situation and to give a new dimension to their lives: the imaginary situation.

Mods are optimists. They behave like winners but in reality, they are losers. They are the bearers of the contemporary euphoria, mythologised by the media and launched in the notion of *Swinging London*[209].

It is worth looking at the relationship between the Mods and the media but, in essence, it does not differ that much from the treatment other youth cultures have received before and since. The media were mostly interested in the sensational

---

[207] Dick Hebdige: The Style of the Mods (Centre for Contemporary Cultural Studies paper, University of Birmingham, 1973) p 9
[208] Dick Hebdige: The Style of the Mods (Centre for Contemporary Cultural Studies paper, University of Birmingham, 1973) p 10
[209] Web: http://boingboing.net/2008/03/11/1966-time-article-ab.html

aspects of the lifestyle: dress, behaviour, violence and drugs, i.e. the usual themes that cause a 'moral panic' among adult society.

> "The fact that Mods and rockers clashed before the camera is, I suspect, more indicative for the Mod's vanity than of any really deeply felt antagonism between the two groups."[210]

The Skinheads[211]

If Cohen portrays Mods as taking the upward option, he then posits the Skinheads as the example of choosing the downward option as a potential answer to the contradictions in the parent culture.

The end of the 1960s are characterised by increasing numbers of immigrants from the Commonwealth, most of which had gained its independence; the ever expanding welfare state with its still badly performing housing policy; and the arrival of Flower Power[212] from America which found fertile ground in Britain too[213].

The rise of the Skinheads is theoretically described as:

> "The magical recovery of the working class community."[214]

Skinheads play on a number of working class themes such as racism, sexism, chauvinism, neighbourhood solidarity and group affiliation. It is remarkable how similar the societal processes are in the Ted, Mod and Skinhead periods: the demolition, literally and metaphorically, of many working

---

[210] Dick Hebdige: The Style of the Mods (Centre for Contemporary Cultural Studies paper, University of Birmingham, 1973) p 4. See also: Stanley Cohen: Folk Devils and Moral Panics, The Creation of the Mods and Rockers (Martin Robertson, Oxford, 1980)
[211] Photo:
http://www.kevinrdshepherd.net/assets/images/early_skinheads.jpg
[212] Web: http://www.hippy.com/60s.htm
[213] Paul Willis: Profane Culture (Routledge & Kegan Paul, London, 1978)
[214] John Clarke: The Skinheads and the Study of Youth Culture (Centre for Contemporary Cultural Studies paper, University of Birmingham, 1973)

Hans Versluys: London's Burning, An Exploration in Punk Subculture
Political & Social Sciences Department, University of Antwerpen, 1980

92

class areas; the introduction of a middle class way of life concentrating on family and home, together with a consumer mindset and an increasing standard of living.

The Skinheads attempted to restore the old values of the lost class solidarity in a symbolic way. Not only by their behaviour in a gang and creating their identity through these group processes but also through a number of activities such as violent attacks on Pakistani immigrants, gays and at football grounds. This violence is interpreted as a reaction to a number of social changes that caused alienation: immigration into traditional working class neighbourhoods, the spread of the middle class (non-macho, perceived effeminate) hippie culture, the professionalisation, internationalisation and commercialisation of football. The working class kid who became a skinhead confronted a middle class invasion of his life experience (the *bourgeoisification* of the working class). This evolutionary change of the bourgeois ethos (consumer, spectator, passivity and rationality) was in direct contradiction to the original working class ethos of participant in, loyal fan and active supporter of and emotionally involved with the favourite football club. For Cohen the fundamental contradiction in the parent culture was:

> "At an ideological level, between traditional working class Puritanism and the new hedonism of consumption."[215]

In their relationship with other subcultures, Skinheads were always very negative in their attitudes. They despised the Hippies for reasons mentioned earlier, and so were the Mods, whom they declared too commercialised and thus irrelevant. The Skinhead movement did get into a rut because it failed to establish links and contacts with other youth groups.
Their violent aspects caused the media to opportunistically spread a moral panic[216] by sensational reportage. But the

---

[215] Phil Cohen: Subcultural Conflict and Working Class Community (Centre for Contemporary Cultural Studies paper, University of Birmingham, 1973)

unwillingness of the Skinheads to assemble more broadly than on a very localised scale (*"London Boot Boys Rule Here"*) inhibited a wide dispersal of their thoughts and subculture. They were basically sunk by their own contradictions.

Joe Strummer of the Clash, Auckland 1982.
Photo © Jonathan Ganley

The Punks

Very few theoretical and scholarly studies are available for our current study of punks, so what follows can be construed as highly speculative. However, we will try to apply logically what has been studied in earlier youth subcultures and keep within their guidance.

Generally, we can state that the economic crisis in the UK started in 1968 when, for the first time in the post-war

---

[216] Stanley Cohen: Folk Devils and Moral Panics, The Creation of the Mods and Rockers (Martin Robertson, Oxford, 1980)

period, supply of labour surpassed its demand[217]. Again, it is clear that the period of economic euphoria promising unlimited growth in the general standard of living, was a myth. The Skinheads reacted already to this fact and the assorted job restructuring into automatisation, which undermined the traditional labour ethos of the working class. In the second half of the 1970s, this crisis deepens and especially hits unskilled youngsters who are being shut out of the labour market except for very demeaning and dead-end jobs. The desperation and frustration caused by these real futureless prospects we already discussed in the ethnographical part.

The extremism in the punk reactions is understandable. Punks explore, not upwards or downwards, but outwards. They unhook themselves from the system, or start an alternative career. If they can only count on society to provide them with a poverty income or a dead-end job, then various options are 'available'. There were those who dropped out but there was no easy place to flee to, no 'punk San Francisco', nor did they have the financial means to start using hard drugs – although some did take this escapist route[218].

Others developed a strong political consciousness, aligned themselves with anarchism and tried to change society through 'undermining' activities. Regarding punk anarchism, we already mentioned that it had a pragmatic streak, focusing more on deeds than words. The 'appropriation' of various means of communication such as the press, record labels, clothes and badges are a reaction to both the alienation of the established media and a reaction to the broader alienation of the working class from its means of expression and organization. Tabloid newspapers, more concerned with scandal and celebrity than news, replaced the labour press; the Labour Party is as much - or as little – reform-minded as the Tories; and in the trade unions too, a

---

[217] Simon Frith: Sociology of Rock (Constable, London, 1978) p 34
[218] Web: http://www.findagrave.com/cgi-bin/fg.cgi?page=gr&GRid=3675

bureaucracy has grown up which leaves little space for individuality.

On top of this, social reactions to the punk styles was so massive and laced with panic they provided the living proof for blame and comments by punks on society's condition and contradictions. The ideological 'tolerance' in sexuality and the explicit repression (not only in a legal sense) of pornography and homosexuality we have already discussed in the chapter on clothing and image. The punks have made this contradiction visible and acted it out to the full.

Although, on an appearance level, punks look completely different from previous subcultures and punks actively deny all those who came before them and want nothing to do with them, it is remarkable how many style elements were adopted from the Teds, Mods, Hippies and Skinheads: punk music has its roots in rock'n'roll, albeit transformed and helped by technological innovations. In clothing too, a number of style elements return such as the *brothel creepers* of the Teds, the tie from the Mods, the leather jackets from the Rockers and Bike Boys (the Mods' counterparts), but everything was reconstructed and selected in extremist forms: the technicolour hair style, the lunatic make up, the garbage clothes.

Other elements adopted were, for example, the ideology of self-expression from – oh, the irony – the Hippies who themselves had borrowed it from classic liberalism[219] and the group unity and identity (sometimes with an associated territoriality - "Harrow Punx" – but this is generally doubtful as it is in contradiction with the punk idea of individuality). Solidarity between punks could be explained as the expression of, and as a reaction to, the lost broad class solidarity and its replacement by 'solidarity within the family'.

---

[219] Geoff Mungham & Geoff Pearson: Working Class Youth Culture (Routledge & Kegan Paul, London, 1977)

Even the aspect of punk violence – strongly exaggerated in the media – can be explained in the same sense, and they do it themselves:

> "We're a generation brought up on the importance of war and romance without having experienced either. Heads full of sterile sex images and sensationalised shock horror [...] Attack Attack Attack [...] with physical control by media. Our emotion can't keep up. Blank generation. Right now, it's not too difficult to identify with Rotten's lyrics. Violence and sex don't mean that much. It's a joke. Self love is the constant theme for survival."
> Al McDowell[220]

Despite all good intentions, statements, explanations and protests in the fanzines, the punk movement was no match for the social control mechanisms, such as the media, the police or the politicians. Its defences were too weak and in a too premature stadium to offer proper nuances to the labeling by the media as 'deviant', 'violent' and 'dirty'. So currently, we are still faced with the stereotype of a violent, uncompromising, annoying and ugly adolescent, typecast as a punk.

---

[220] Isabelle Anscombe: Not Another Punk Book (Aurum, London, 1978) p 70

3.4   Evaluation of the Responses

The main conclusion to remember is that every subculture solves its problems in an 'imaginary' way, a way that does not tackle the fundamentals of its problems, but transforms them and expresses and lives them out symbolically, but also truly.

A subculture is, as mentioned before, one possible response by a working class young person to his situation - another one could be, for instance, developing a revolutionary consciousness.
The adoption of a particular response is dependent on time and social circumstances, such as the social and cultural environment; the economic situation and expectations; changes in the physical world and technological innovations. The working class young person and his response to his situation still has a relationship with the adult world and its ideologies, class structures and class cultures, and with other young people who opted for a different response.
Various solutions are possible, which means each is relative, and each has its faults and weaknesses.
We will now look at the specific weaknesses and problems in the subcultural responses and solutions.

As the name suggests, subcultures operate on a 'cultural' level. This means that their main focus is on the development of a 'way of life', a symbolic attempt to solve problems by the development of a style, a behaviour, an ideology, a belief, means of communications and a number of rules and underlying references (in sociological jargon, values and norms).

The subcultural response is not simply ideological but also real. Hall and Jefferson call this 'space winning'[221]: a territorial definition of a space by young people where outsiders are unwanted. We already discussed how music is a

---

[221] Stuart Hall & Tony Jefferson: Resistance Through Rituals, Youth Subcultures in Post-War Britain (Hutchinson, London, 1977) p 35

good, but albeit limited, 'border guard' to keep out, for example, adults.
This solution and territorial defence is exceptionally limited. Society, in the guise of the record industry, the SPG[222] (Special Patrol Group) and officially sanctioned youth clubs, succeeds in invading from all sides and in integrating all the attainments of the subculture successfully into its own systems. The music industry is the most remarkable example of this, but also the creation of youth clubs with their informal mechanisms to control can be seen in this light. Teddy Boys, for instance, absolutely hated them.

A youth culture is but one limited solution for youth problems. It limits itself mainly to one sphere of life, i.e. leisure time, and even there it cannot match the interventions by society. Subcultures have no, or only very limited, solutions for their problems that really matter in the social and economic spheres of life: unemployment, educational under-achievement and dead-end jobs.

For a minority a subculture can offer an alternative career but that is doubtful for the majority: only a small number of people will have a legendary career in football or rock'n'roll.
Only those spheres where punk action transcended the leisure sphere, such as the production of a fanzine or the setting up of a record label, offered a real opportunity to improve the youngsters' situation.
But, as we have seen before, we must add nuances to them and point to their limited influence. Capitalist economic laws apply also to those enterprises, which are as such no alternative to the capitalist mode of production and its production and consumption spiral. Only the Hippies have in a limited way attempted to set up an alternative production and distribution system, but even they have not succeeded in replacing purchasing power as the origin of production and distribution of goods and services.

---

[222] Web: http://www.met.police.uk/history/special_patrol.htm

Subcultures offered to their members little more than an 'imaginary' solution. The lack of status of the Teddy Boys is 'compensated' by dressing in upper-class clothes at the weekend. The 'fetishisation of style' and consumption by the Mods bridges the chasm between the never-ending weekend and the grey Monday morning. Skinheads 'revalue' the archetypal working class values through the 'conquest' of a territory taken away from them by urban planners, 'identification' with a football team and the 'representation' of the traditional labourers' look. Then the punks who express the frustration about the promised welfare state in an extreme parody of the social norms such as beauty, style, virtuosity, originality, sensuality, community and hedonism, alongside the 'reconquista' of music and ideas.

3.5   Social Reactions to Youth Cultures

In subcultural history, the supervising state has never been absent or has tolerated everything what subcultures got up to. The dominant culture has always had an interest in and a real influence on the development of subcultures. We will attempt to trace the interventions.

First, there is the commercial interest in the cultural products and symbols generated by the subcultures. Music, clothing design, appearance and publications are, due to their physical existence, extremely suitable to be adopted as sellable products by industry. Record companies, fashion and clothing retailers, and publishers profit from, and depend in large extent on what young people generate. For example, in the rock music business it has been proven time after time that a new rock variant or fashion trend only hits the mark, i.e. is worthwhile to be exploited commercially, when a minimal need exists amongst the public, but innovative needs are difficult to manufacture:

> "Musical innovations always come from outside the major record companies"[223]

Secondly, and no less important are the post-war social, ethical and political reactions to the phenomenon of youth. This is called a 'moral panic'[224] and it has accompanied every youth culture since the war. The Centre for Contemporary Cultural Studies in Birmingham[225] has researched this phenomenon in depth in the 1970s.

---

[223] Simon Frith: Sociology of Rock (Constable, London, 1978) p 101. See also Dave Laing: The Sound of Our Time (Sheed & Ward, London, 1969) and Richard Middleton: Pop Music and The Blues (Gollancz, London, 1972) for more commentary on this aspect.
[224] Stanley Cohen: Folk Devils and Moral Panics, The Creation of the Mods and Rockers (Martin Robertson, Oxford, 1980)
[225] Web: http://www.jahsonic.com/CCCS.html

The main point is that social interest in youth is rooted in the notion that 'youth' symbolises change in society: the 'new times' of abundance and high standards of living for everybody with youth as the hedonistic, carefree, classless, consuming 'new man', created in the welfare state. This 'new times mentality' indicate an implicit loss and discounting of old, established structures, definitions and patterns of life. Hall and Jefferson argue[226] this happened alongside a societal anxiousness for the new, unknown and uncertain future.

When this 'new society' is already being 'lived' by a number of subcultures offering new interpretations relating to their situations, this elicits a direct spur to defend, via a moral panic, the original positions and power structures against this invasion of 'new definitions'. Youth cultures in all their aspects are seen as a direct threat to existing authorities. Delinquency and aggression especially were the focus of public curiosity, although public discourse 'analysed' and commented on their sartorial styles and ways of life in general too. Remember the extensive reporting on every incident during punk gigs or the battles between 'rival' youth gangs and subcultures, and the reportage on punk in almost every self-respecting illustrated magazine in Britain and abroad.

The subcultures discussed here all appeared during crucial moments in history, during periods of profound social change: the Teds at the birth of the welfare state; the Mods during the Cold War and the start of the Swinging Sixties; the Skinheads at the rise of the multi-racial society; and the Punks in the depression.
In contrast, the media looking for the causation of the working class subcultures were labeling it more under the rubric of 'civil unrest'[227], while considering a middle class

---

[226] Stuart Hall & Tony Jefferson: Resistance Through Rituals, Youth Subcultures in Post-War Britain (Hutchinson, London, 1977)
[227] Stuart Hall & Tony Jefferson: Resistance Through Rituals, Youth Subcultures in Post-War Britain (Hutchinson, London, 1977) p 72

subculture like the Hippies more as a deliberate undermining of society with the Hippies playing the role of agents of social destruction.

When punk also added political issues to the 'way-of-life' agenda, such as 'Anarchy', 'freedom' or 'right to work', they were labeled as a subversive minority and heavy countermeasures (as during the St Paul's riot[228] in Bristol at Easter 1980) were applied. Smaller annoying actions and boycotts were successful but in some instances had a contrary effect: the ban on punk gigs, the ban on radio play and the boycott by venue owners created new meeting places and record labels.

The social boycott of the punk phenomenon, taken together with a public interest in it, was a two-sided sword. It was both an effective 'neutraliser' – by diverting attention away from punk criticisms and focusing only on the fashion styles and appearances – and a stimulator to go further and do more, like setting up a record label or designing politically more extreme points of view: not only musical anarchy but also political anarchism.

This ambiguity of simultaneous disgust and fascination for subcultures by the media is not new, nor exclusive towards punk. The Mods, Hippies and others all had their media treatments. The CCCS even suggests that law changes in the public order area are proof of attempts to better control any young people who question and undermine existing power structures. Youth regarded as the 'Devil', the 'Enemy', and the 'Anarchists'[229]. Recent announcements (such as the Public Order Act 1980) by the Conservative Government to clamp down, to detain young criminals more readily and stricter controls on 'hooligan' violence at football grounds, can be regarded as panic reactions by a society that doesn't succeed

---

[228] Web: http://discoveringbristol.org.uk/browse/slavery/st-pauls-riots-smashed-car-window/
[229] Stuart Hall & Tony Jefferson: Resistance Through Rituals, Youth Subcultures in Post-War Britain (Hutchinson, London, 1977) p 74

in getting the young on 'its side'. The state regards young people a nightmare for the existing order and authority and as a physical expression of the contradictions in its own ideology of social and economic progress.

CONCLUSION
Problems That Need Solving by Youth Cultures

Each youth culture is embedded in a network of a variety of social forces, institutions and other cultures. At no time is it disconnected from societal structures, although a certain degree of autonomy can be achieved.

Punk has had to deal with, just like all its predecessors, this society, which has an intense interest in what is happening among its youngest members.
Its reaction to the development of deviant and separate subcultures among young people has been up to now in all cases effective: the potentially revolutionary and undermining activities have all been rendered more or less neuter.

The first way was ideological: punk was labeled as a stereotype, as aggressive, violent, dirty, worthless, subversive, arrogant and ruthless. The punk bands, the fans, the look and the pose were extremely visible and easy targets for the media. The underlying motives of boredom and alienation were mentioned but not pointed to as social pathologies, i.e. caused by the social structures themselves. Instead, punk was portrayed as a fashion, a "flash in the pan"[230] and as a "temporary phenomenon"[231]. Nowhere was it taken seriously or no-one predicted a great future for it.

The sensationalisation of punk is a beautiful example of how to turn youth into a symptom and scapegoat for all social problems[232].
Punk life was made difficult by all sides. The media labeled it criminal. Politicians ordered a boycott of public performances and cut the number of meeting places (The ban on open air

---

[230] Tijdschrift voor Diplomatie, 1978, p 442
[231] Sunday Times, November 1976
[232] Stuart Hall & Tony Jefferson: Resistance Through Rituals, Youth Subcultures in Post-War Britain (Hutchinson, London, 1977)

gigs by The Buzzcocks in the Summer of 1979, and the loudly protested and resisted closure of the Beaufort Market on the King's Road in 1979[233]). Emotional media reactions have influenced, if not determined, political decisions (e.g. the Thames TV incident) and the music industry was quickly on the ball to exploit it financially and commercially.

These attacks in the ideological, political and commercial spheres were too strong and the defence strategies of the punk movement too weak, or even non-existent. The fundamental weakness of subcultures in general, their too-limited field of action in the leisure sphere only, is only partially applicable to punk, but the promising developments in production are still too minimal and not alternative enough to be able to match the existing structures.
However, is a subculture capable of doing that?

We have seen that youth, and in particular, working class youth is in a double subordinate position in relation to the working class culture and the dominant culture.
In punk's case, it could not count on the active support of the parent culture in its attempts to appropriate what was alienated. The media played a crucial role in this process too: 'normal', 'healthy' and 'commonsensical' parents were paraded (in the form of letters to the editor) to not only dismiss the punk phenomenon, but to also demand concrete measures to limit and eliminate it (e.g. the reactions to the Thames TV broadcast).

This battle over 'space winning', labeling and commercial exploitation was fought in an arena between two unequal parties. Only with the active solidarity of the parent culture and other youth cultures, together with a 'radical' programme containing more than just culturally living out your situation, punk will be able to become a real threat to the existing establishments it wants to kick against.

---

[233] in: New Musical Express, 7 April 1979

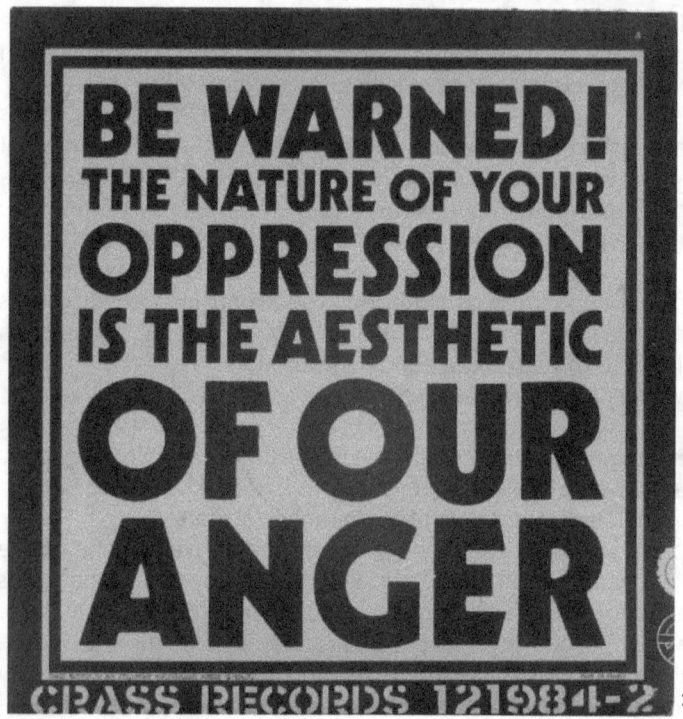

[234]

---

[234] Crass record, 1983

ANNEXES (blogs and essays)

The 31 October 1980 Riot Wilrijk (Belgium)[235]

I had almost forgotten about it, but 31 October is kind of a special night in my biography and not for any pagan ritualistic reasons to dress up and scare the locals (I don't need an excuse of Halloween for that).

On 31 October 1980, a few mates and I organised a punk rock festival at a local youth club, called *Djevano*, in a very middle class Catholic suburb. Belgian and Dutch bands were scheduled to gig (Spermicide, Noise Boys 906, Ze Barbies, Soviet Sex and De Brassers) but within an hour the local citizenry were alerted to and alarmed by the display and parade of about a thousand technicolour-haired, leather-clad punks of indeterminate gender. (As was the fashion then - I remember wearing a white wool ski-jumper, I mean, I wanted to stand out from the black-attired crowds!).
The cops were duly called and they arrived in a few VW-combi-vans.
In the middle of a set, one burly law enforcement officer took to the stage to declare the proceedings over. I'm not sure what they teach these guys in cop school about handling crowds of a subculturally, shall we say, volatile nature. But the reaction from the amassed crowds, many of whom came from a large area of Western Europe for the occasion (the event had been publicised in a large number of fanzines, what with no internet and all), was rather irate.

So it all ended in tears: chairs were thrown onto the stage, the cops retreated with batons drawn, clubbing their way out, grabbing a few punters left and right and dragging them into their combi-vans, which by this stage had been reduced to window-less and smashed-up motorised pig-crates. The

---

[235] Blog 31 October 2005: http://uroskin.blogspot.com/2005/10/i-had-almost-forgotten-about-it-but-31.html

suburbs had never seen such a display of the stiff arm of the law meeting the unmovable force of speedy punks on a high.

White Riot indeed.

It, of course, made the papers the next day, but at the time I was unaware of the damage caused outside the club, since I was busy clearing up the debris inside as every youth club committee member was wont to do at the end of each night.
Two days later, I was summoned to the cop shop for a statement. My sociological explanations of the happenings (I had freshly graduated three months before and keen as to display my research findings - I had done, after all, my thesis on punk rock) seemed to interest the duty sergeant. But his supervisor, who was sitting in on our interview, just went from ginger to red to beetroot in the face the longer I went on. There was some thumb thumping, shouting and general frustration all-round, but in the end they had to let me go even after threatening to sue for damage caused to their beloved cattle trucks. Of course, nothing came of that, but I guess they really had to cover their cop arse: several punks randomly arrested on the night were fined, even though it was completely impossible to find those responsible for the damage caused.

In the end, the youth club, where I had been hanging out and working for six years, cancelled my organising committee membership, but I was not banned from the premises. The club soon after closed for good.
The night was also, auspiciously, Radio Centraal's first broadcast night[236]. I worked there for six years and my media career was born.

---

[236] Official site: http://www.radiocentraal.be/Realescape/

The death of Malcolm McLaren[237]

Malcolm McLaren, patron saint of rock band public relations publicists and managers, Chelsea's version of the Wizard of Oz, cultural revolutionary and Situationist iconoclast, has died[238].

I have never met the man, but have always been amused by his tactics of getting up the noses of many in the establishment, from ITV hacks, Royal Jubilee organisers, tabloid newspaper editors and record company execs to even his former protégé, John Lydon.
He was always worth listening to, his cutting commentary on contemporary culture was always wry and biting. They could barely shut him up when he was on the radio or in nostalgic punk rock documentaries!

Of course, he didn't invent punk rock nor was its midwife and nanny, but you can't help but think subcultural history would have been different, much less infused with a 1968 ethos, if he hadn't been there. I would like to remember him as the Daniel Cohn-Bendit of punk, channeling the zeitgeist of the late 1970s and nurturing it into something we can still feel vibrate today.

---

[237] Blog 9 April 2010: http://uroskin.blogspot.com/2010/04/malcolm-mclaren-1946-2010.html
[238] News report: http://news.bbc.co.uk/2/hi/uk_news/8610423.stm

Hans Versluys: London's Burning, An Exploration in Punk Subculture
Political & Social Sciences Department, University of Antwerpen, 1980

110

Rough Trade[239]

> *"At a time when CD price wars and music downloads are putting entire High Street chains at risk, independent retailers Rough Trade are opening what they say is the country's biggest music-only specialist store.*
> *[...] The first Rough Trade shop opened in Notting Hill, west London, in 1976, and soon became known as one of the best places to find new wave music and fanzines.*
> *A record label of the same name followed, but the two businesses went their separate ways in 1982 and are now run independently of each other."*
> (BBC News[240])

I remember visiting the Rough Trade shop in Notting Hill many times during my frequent pilgrimage trips to London as a wide-eyed innocent punk rocker in the late 1970s. It was just the most magical shop where the reggae and punk rock 7-inch singles sounds wafted out of the shop as if it was Notting Hill Carnival time permanently. Not only the music was important. Also the piles and piles of fanzines and badges. Every punk rocker worth his second-hand clothes and hairstyle either played in a band or published a fanzine (sometimes both) and none would be complete without lapels full of badges.

Reading about Rough Trade always makes me quite nostalgic. I still have a pile of Rough Trade singles and fanzines (the badges seem to have gone AWOL while moving between countries and continents).

---

[239] Blog 19 July 2007: http://uroskin.blogspot.com/2007/07/rough-trade.html
[240] News report: http://news.bbc.co.uk/2/hi/business/6903052.stm

The death of the single[241]

I found an interesting essay in, of all places, the Daily Torygraph[242] on the demise of the single record.

> *"The art of the single was never really about the song. It was about the trouble you took to find it, the walk to the record shop and the effort involved in copying the lead singer's hairstyle."*

Searching, finding and buying a 7-inch record was always about more than just the pop song that it contained. It was a pure fetishistic pleasure contained in the package - the more outlandish the format/sleeve art the cooler! Remember all that coloured vinyl (white was always my favourite); the textured sleeves; the double hole in the record the band Non on Mute Records[243] so you could play it elliptically at all speeds too; the Public Image Limited newspaper sleeve wrapped around their first single:

---

[241] Blog 2 February 2005: http://uroskin.blogspot.com/2005/02/death-of-single-via-jockohomo.html
[242] http://www.telegraph.co.uk/culture/music/3635867/The-sad-death-of-the-pop-single.html
[243] http://www.discogs.com/NON-Smegma-Split/release/205468

(No, you can't make me an offer, I would rather sell my boyfriend instead!); the British small holes compared to the continental big ones (stop sniggering, in record hole divisions, smaller was always far cooler than big); picture sleeves which were always special in the UK while it was standard issue on the continent.

I got obsessed by some small record labels, such as Rough Trade and Small Wonder Records (and even Mute), and collected them as much as I could. 25 years later, I still got them all.

It all went wrong when record companies discovered all these goodies could be used as vile marketing tools to extract coin from punters who simply had to have everything that was released by their favourite pop star. Now everything comes down from your computer to your i(diot)-pod in one easily-charged-for file. Boy, am I glad I don't have to be young these days.

Punk: Attitude - a documentary by Don Letts[244]

"Punk: Attitude" is a rich cornucopia of sound bites by a huge coterie of ageing punk rockers from the early 1970s to the almost present, with a, to my mind, biased slant towards American bands and a less than subtle snub to the British punk rockers.

It was telling that many an essential mover and shaker at the time, such as John Lydon, Malcolm McLaren and Vivienne Westwood, were all missing from the interviews. Which was kind of a shame and it was left unexplained.
But it was good to hear it confirmed, even if this is a somewhat uncharitable take on it, that UK punk rock was killed off by Americans on smack - the hippies' revenge?
Don Letts made the excellent *"The Punk Rock Movie"*[245] in 1978, which was actually a far more interesting look at the contemporary subcultural phenomenon than this 2005 'update'.

But it was fun to see all those aged, balding wrinklies (pretty much what I stare at in the mirror in the morning too), but the women still looked excellent: Siouxsie Sioux, Chrissie Hynde and, especially, the ever-wonderful Poly Styrene and Ari Up.
There are quite a few memorable quotes (and David Johansen has to be seen to be believed). My favourite came from Henry Rollins when commenting on the "hardcore punk" scene that came after as:

> *"Guys touching each other, sweating, flesh, pectoral muscles. Very homo-erotic. You say, fellas, stop fighting. Get a room. Get it over with."*

---

[244] Blog 26 October 2006 http://uroskin.blogspot.com/2006/10/punk-attitude.html
[245] Video: http://video.google.com/videoplay?docid=4101813390428941237#

A funny thing happened to me on the road to the Buzzcocks[246]

It must be a sign of my mid-life crisis that I was rather looking forward to going to the Buzzcocks, a punk band I never managed to see first time around in 1977, but I have always liked since that *Spiral Scratch* EP. Now they were playing in Auckland on a comeback tour, so that would make a good birthday present to myself.

Walking up Queen Street to the venue, I was accosted by that perennial gauntlet of Hara Krishna devotees, who, when not chanting and singing on Friday nights, try to engage you in conversation to sell you some of their books. This particular one who latched on to me wasn't half bad looking so I thought, why not play a little game with him to amuse myself.
This is how the conversation went:

> *The monk: "Hello, can I ask you a question?"*
> *Me: "Sure you can."*
> *The Monk: "What do you do in your life?"*
> *Me: "I'm a faggot."*
> *The Monk (visibly uncomfortable and squirming):*
> *"Professionally?"*
> *(He obviously knew the word and what it meant, even*
> *though I hear Hare Krishnas are supposed to have no sex*
> *lives)*
> *Me: "No, it's my hobby."*
> *(I swear I saw him blush, he avoided any further eye*
> *contact and didn't persist in questioning me any further on*
> *it.)*
> *The Monk: "I see we have similar hair styles" (and took his*
> *cap off revealing his shaved skull with a little rat-tail hair-*
> *do)*

I pondered about asking him out on a date but I just knew that would have been a step too far. Instead, we chatted

---

[246] Blog 18 September 2006: http://uroskin.blogspot.com/2006/09/funny-thing-happened-to-me-on-road-to.html

about the Hara Krishna restaurant on K Road, which, incidentally, I can heartily recommend if you want some healthy fast food. I made my excuse to leave and he never even bothered to try to sell me any of his tracts.

The Buzzcocks, by the way, were a whole load of nostalgic singalong fun. Just like they used to be. I prayed Pete Shelley would sing "Homo Sapien", but that was as likely as laying the monk.

Generation Knows Nowt[247]

This week's episode of "*South Park*" on C4 was one of the weakest I have seen. It just didn't make any sense and it wasn't even funny.

The premise was that when a Woodstock-type revivalist concert is being held in town, the resident vigilante Eric Cartman made it his mission to kill all the hippies - even without the help of the two Vietnam vets, who, in their time actually would have killed some, given half a chance. The Woodstock generation reviving their youth is now all in their sixties and therefore would not have sons in the 8th grade, like our cartoon heroes. Instead, the hippies would have been their grandparents, despite most parents in South Park looking suspiciously aged. I guess it's a case of Parker & Stone rebelling against their own parents, sort of 40 years later. And Slayer or any other death metal music didn't kill any hippies, what sort of distorted subcultural history is that?

No, to its credit, C4 provided the right answer after South Park on the same night: the episode of the "*Classic Albums*" series featured "*Never Mind the Bollocks*" by The Sex Pistols, hippie killers par excellence, and not so much an album as a Communist Manifesto-esque death knell to mid-1970s rock music.

Hippie drugs like heroin did kill some punks, Sid Vicious among them, but then that Spungen woman - and by extension American drug culture - was the hand behind that. John Lydon was gloriously funny, as ever, and still sarcastically biting on Malcolm McLaren, but overall all the punks seemed to have mellowed in old age (see Julie Burchill). I even notice that when looking at myself in the mirror.

---

[247] Blog 17 February 2006: http://uroskin.blogspot.com/2006/02/generation-knows-nowt-this-weeks.html

John Peel (1939-2004)[248]

The thing about John Peel was that he made you listen to new, unusual and idiosyncratic music and you felt better, culturally, for it afterwards.
He liked to challenge your tastes and seduce you to appreciate new work, not because it was new, but because you could trust him to have listened with a critical ear beforehand and that it had passed muster.

My first memory of listening to the John Peel show was in bed, under the covers, with my little transistor radio tuned to BBC Radio 1 in 1977. His was a late night show and medium wave radio from Britain only reached my home town on the continent after dark. So it was an ideal introduction to new music and it certainly shaped my taste as a rookie punk rocker at the time.
His soundtrack of punk rock and reggae alternating and playing off against each other I thought was marvellous and the nightclub I spent my youth in (Cinderella's Ballroom in Antwerpen) adopted this mix of then contemporary underground music. It was hilarious and rousing. Of course, it changed my life and I didn't want to miss one second of it.

Thanks for the excitement, Mr Peel, and if God is a DJ, he must have learned all the tricks from you.

Addendum: In 2002, John Peel came to New Zealand, nay, he even stayed on Waiheke Island and he said[249]:

> *"This might be the loveliest place I've ever been."*

---

[248] Blog 27 October 2004: http://uroskin.blogspot.com/2004/10/john-peel-1939-2004-thing-about-john.html
[249] http://www.telegraph.co.uk/culture/music/3626222/Youre-a-god-I-said.-He-took-it-very-well.html

24 Hour Party People[250]

When watching *"24 Hour Party People"* last night I thought
what an unsung hero Tony Wilson, who set up Factory
Records, has been in the punk/post-punk era.
The kind of self-help/co-operative structure of his ventures
has always been the essence of the punk ethos and, quoted in
the film, he never sold out because he had never anything to
sell.

I think modern music's history would have been much poorer
without Factory Records.
Joy Division and New Order are treasures. *"Love Will Tear Us
Apart"*[251] (FAC 23) is the best single ever.
Ian Curtis is still very much missed and Sean Harris was
brilliant in his role in the film.
Vinni Reilly (Durutti Column[252]) was the sweetest Factory pop
star of them all.
I never cared much about the 'Madchester' scene or all that
drug-fuelled raving and I never went to The Hacienda (FAC
51).
It was a lot of fun trying to collect all Factory label products
numbers[253], which must be the Aspie in me.

---

[250] Blog 8 June 2004: http://uroskin.blogspot.com/2004/06/watched-24-hour-party-people-last.html
[251] Lyrics:
http://www.davemcnally.com/lyrics/JoyDivision/LoveWillTearUsApart.asp
[252] Official site: http://www.thedurutticolumn.com/
[253] Unofficial archive: http://www.cerysmaticfactory.info/index.html

LITERATURE: BOOKS

AH Hanson & Malcolm Wallis: Governing Britain (Fontana, Glasgow, 1978)

AJP Taylor: Revolutions and Revolutionaries (Atheneum, New York, 1980)

AJP Taylor: Essays in English History (Penguin, Harmondsworth, 1976)

Alistair Beaton & Andy Hamilton: The Secret Thatcher Papers (New English Library, London, 1980)

Ann Barr & Peter York: The Official Sloane Ranger Handbook (Ebury Press, London, 1982)

Arthur Marwick: British Society Since 1945 (Pelican, Harmondsworth, 1982)

Attila The Stockbroker & Seething Wells: The Rising Sons of Ranting Verse (Unwin, London, 1985)

Brian Jackson & Dennis Marsden: Education and the Working Class (Pelican, Harmondsworth, 1975)

Caroline Coon: 1988 The New Wave Punk Rock Explosion (Orbach & Chambers, London, 1977)

Charles Poulsen: The English Rebels (Journeyman Press, London, 1984)

Clifford Adelman: Generations, A Collage on Youthcult (Pelican, Harmondsworth, 1973)

Colin MacInnes: Absolute Beginners (Allison & Busby, London, 1959)

Colin MacInnes: City of Spades (Allison & Busby, London, 1957)

Colin MacInnes: Mr Love and Mr Justice (Allison & Busby, London, 1960)

Dave Laing: The Sound of Our Time (Sheed & Ward, London, 1969)

David Robbins & Philip Cohen: Knuckle Sandwich, Growing Up in the Working Class City (Penguin, Harmondsworth, 1978)

Derek Jarman: Dancing Ledge (Quartet, London, 1984)

Derek Jarman: Of Angels & Apocalypse (Afterimage, London, 1985)

Derek Jarman: The Last of England (Constable, London, 1987)

Deyan Sudjic: Cult Heroes: How to be Famous for more than Fifteen Minutes (WW Norton, New York, 1989)

Dick Hebdige: Subculture, The Meaning of Style (Methuen, London, 1979)

Eric Butterworth & David Weir: Sociology of Modern Britain (Fontana, Glasgow, 1978)

Fred & Judy Vermorel: The Sex Pistols (Tandem, London, 1978)

Fred Inglis: Radical Earnestness, English Social Theory 1880-1980 (Martin Robertson, Oxford, 1982)

Gareth Steadman Jones: Outcast London, A Study in the Relationship between Classes in Victorian Society (Penguin, Harmondsworth, 1971)

Geoff Mungham & Geoff Pearson: Working Class Youth Culture (Routledge & Kegan Paul, London, 1977)

Gert Peelen: Van Verlossing tot Vertrossing (Anthos, Baarn, 1976)

Greil Marcus: Lipstick Traces, A Secret History of the Twentieth Century (Secker & Warburg, London, 1989)

Guido De Corte, Universiteit Antwerpen, Department Didaktiek en Kritiek, lecture notes, 1980

Guy Debord: De spektakelmaatschappij (Het Wereldvenster, Baarn, 1976)

Hans Ferree: Van mens tot marionet (Spectrum, Utrecht, 1978)

Harold Wilson: The Governance of Britain (Weidenfeld & Nicolson, London, 1976)

Harry Hoefnagels: Sociologie en maatschappijkritiek (Samson, Alphen, 1972)

Henry Sloane: Sloane's Inside Guide to Sex & Drugs & Rock'n'Roll (Pan Books, London, 1985)

Herman Deleeck: Ongelijkheden in de welvaartstaat (De Nederlandsche Boekhandel, Antwerpen, 1977)

Ian Birch: The Book With No Name (Omnibus Press, London, 1980)

Isabelle Anscombe: Not Another Punk Book (Aurum, London, 1978)

James Coleman: The Adolescent Society (The Free Press, Glencoe, Il, 1961)

James Patrick: A Glasgow Gang Observed (Eyre Methuen, London, 1973)

Jasper Ridley: The History of England (Futura, London, 1981)

JFC Harrison: The Common People (Fontana, London, 1984)

John Kenneth Galbraith: The Age of Uncertainty (BBC/Andre Deutsch, London, 1977)

John Waters: Shock Value, A Tasteful Book About Bad Taste (Delta, New York, 1981)

John Tobler: Punk Rock (Phoebus, London, 1977)

Jon Savage: England's Dreaming, The Sex Pistols and Punk Rock (Faber & Faber, 1991)

Jon Savage: Time Travel, From the Sex Pistols to Nirvana: Pop, Media and Sexuality, 1977-96 (Chatto & Windus, London, 1996)

Julie Burchill: Sex and Sensibility (Grafton, London, 1992)

Julie Burchill & Tony Parsons: The Boy Looked At Johnny, The Obituary of Rock and Roll (Pluto Press, London, 1978)

Kevin Hawkins: Unemployment (Pelican, Harmondsworth, 1979)

Louis van Bladel: De kerngedachten van Karl Marx (De Nederlandsche Boekhandel, 1976)

Mark Abrams: Teenage Consumer Spending in 1959 (London Press Exchange, 1961)

Martin Walker: The National Front (Fontana, Glasgow, 1978)

Michael Ball, Fred Fray & Linda McDowell: The Transformation of Britain, Contemporary Social and Economic Change (Fontana, London, 1989)

Michael Dempsey: The Bible, Compilation of Sniffin' Glue (Big O, London, 1978)

Michael Shanks: The Stagnant Society (Penguin, Harmondsworth, 1961)

Michael Young & Peter Wilmott: Family and Kinship in East London (Routledge & Kegan Paul, London, 1969)

Mike Brake: The Sociology of Youth Culture and Youth Subcultures (Routledge & Kegan Paul, London, 1980)

Paul Willis: Learning to Labour (Saxon House, Farnborough, 1977)

Paul Willis: Profane Culture (Routledge & Kegan Paul, London, 1978)

RS Sayers: A History of Economic Change in England 1880-1939 (Oxford University Press, Oxford, 1978)

Ray Stevenson: The Sex Pistols File (Panda, Haverhill, 1978)

Richard Allen: Punk Rock (New English Library, London, 1977)

Richard Lawton & Colin Pooley: Britain 1740-1950, An Historical Geography (Edward Arnold, London, 1992)

Richard Middleton: Pop Music and The Blues (Gollancz, London, 1972)

Simon Frith & Andrew Goodwin (editors): On Record, Rock, Pop & The Written Word, (Pantheon Books, New York, 1990)

Simon Frith: Sociology of Rock (Constable, London, 1978)

Stanley Cohen: Folk Devils and Moral Panics, The Creation of the Mods and Rockers (Martin Robertson, Oxford, 1980)

Stephen Bayley: Taste, The Secret Meaning of Things (Faber & Faber, London, 1991)

Stuart Hall & Tony Jefferson: Resistance Through Rituals, Youth Subcultures in Post-War Britain (Hutchinson, London, 1977)

Theodore Roszak: De opkomst van een tegencultuur (Meulenhoff, Amsterdam, 1976) Translation of: The Making of a Counter Culture: Reflections on the Technocratic Society and Its Youthful Opposition (1968)

Tony Jasper: British Record Charts 1955-1979 (Futura, London, 1979)

Tony Palmer: All You Need Is Love, The Story of Popular Music (Futura, London, 1976)

Val Hennessy: In The Gutter (Quartet, London, 1978)

Virginia Boston: Shockwave (Plexus, London, 1978)

Vita Miezitis: Nightdancin' (Ballantine, New York, 1980)

Walter De Brouwer: Geschiedenis van de kleine man (BRT Open School, Brussel, 1983)

Will Hutton: The State We're In (Vintage, London, 1996)

LITERATURE: PAPERS

Birmingham Community Development Project: Youth on the Dole, Final Report 4 (Social Evaluation Unit, University of Oxford, 1977)

Bob Lumley: Gramsci's Writing on the State and Hegemony, 1916-35 (Centre for Contemporary Cultural Studies paper, University of Birmingham, 1977)

Brian Roberts: Parent and Youth Culture (Centre for Contemporary Cultural Studies paper, University of Birmingham, 1973)

Bryn Jones: The Politics of Popular Culture (Centre for Contemporary Cultural Studies paper, University of Birmingham, 1972)

Chas Critcher: Football since the War: Study in Social Change and Popular Culture (Centre for Contemporary Cultural Studies paper, University of Birmingham, 1974)

Dick Bradley: The Cultural Study of Music: A Theoretical and Methodological Introduction (Centre for Contemporary Cultural Studies paper, University of Birmingham, 1980)

Dick Hebdige: Sub-Cultural Conflict and Criminal Performance in Fulham (Centre for Contemporary Cultural Studies paper, University of Birmingham, 1974)

Dick Hebdige: The Kray Twins: A Study of the System of Closure (Centre for Contemporary Cultural Studies paper, University of Birmingham, 1974)

Dick Hebdige: The Style of the Mods (Centre for Contemporary Cultural Studies paper, University of Birmingham, 1973)

Gary Clarke: Defending Ski Jumpers: A Critique of Theories of Youth Subculture (Centre for Contemporary Cultural Studies paper, University of Birmingham, 1982)

John Clarke & Tony Jefferson: Politics and Popular Culture, Culture and Sub-Culture (Centre for Contemporary Cultural Studies paper, University of Birmingham, 1974)

John Clarke: Football Hooliganism and the Skinheads (Centre for Contemporary Cultural Studies paper, University of Birmingham, 1973)

John Clarke: Newsmaking and Crime (paper at NACRO conference) (Centre for Contemporary Cultural Studies paper, University of Birmingham, 1975)

John Clarke: The Skinheads and the Study of Youth Culture (Centre for Contemporary Cultural Studies paper, University of Birmingham, 1974)

John Clarke: The Three Rs: Repression, Rescue and Rehabilitation - Ideologies of Control for Working Class Youth (Centre for Contemporary Cultural Studies paper, University of Birmingham, 1975)

Julian Tanner: New Directions for Subcultural Theory, an Analysis of British Working-Class Youth Culture (Youth & Society, 1978, 9, 4, June, p 343-372)

Mark Sprangers: De fonografische subindustrie in Belgie (Katholieke Universiteit Leuven, licentiaatsthesis, Leuven, 1982)

Paul Willis: How Working Class Kids get Working Class Jobs (Centre for Contemporary Cultural Studies paper, University of Birmingham, 1975)

Paul Willis: Human Experience and Material Production: Shop Floor Culture (Centre for Contemporary Cultural Studies paper, University of Birmingham, 1975)

Paul Willis: Symbolism and Practice: A Theory for the Social Meaning of Pop Music (Centre for Contemporary Cultural Studies paper, University of Birmingham)

Paul Willis: Symbolism and Practice: The Social Meaning of Pop Music (Centre for Contemporary Cultural Studies paper, University of Birmingham, 1974)

Paul Willis: The Main Reality: Transition School/Work; SSRC Report (Centre for Contemporary Cultural Studies paper, University of Birmingham, 1975)

Paul Willis: Transition from School to Work Bibliography (Centre for Contemporary Cultural Studies paper, University of Birmingham, 1973)

Phil Cohen: Subcultural Conflict and Working Class Community (Centre for Contemporary Cultural Studies paper, University of Birmingham, 1973)

Richard Johnson: Three Problematics: Elements of a Theory of Working Class Culture (Centre for Contemporary Cultural Studies paper, University of Birmingham, 1979)

Stuart Hall: Deviancy, Politics and the Media (Centre for Contemporary Cultural Studies paper, University of Birmingham)

Stuart Hall: The Hippies: An American Moment (Centre for Contemporary Cultural Studies paper, University of Birmingham, 1968)

Tony Jefferson & John Clarke: Down these Mean Streets - The Meaning of Mugging (Centre for Contemporary Cultural Studies paper, University of Birmingham, 1973)

Tony Jefferson & John Clarke: Working Class Youth Cultures (Centre for Contemporary Cultural Studies paper, University of Birmingham, 1973)

Tony Jefferson: The Teds: a Political Resurrection (Centre for Contemporary Cultural Studies paper, University of Birmingham, 1973)

Yves Aerden: Tussen Anarchie en Hysterie: De Punkbeweging in Belgie (1976-1981) (Katholieke Universiteit Leuven, licentiaatsthesis, 2008)

LITERATURE: MAGAZINE ARTICLES

Adrian Thrills: Delta 5, Rock & Roll Rants & The Personal Dance (New Musical Express, 15 March 1980)

Allan Jones: Radio Times, Why Peel Went Punk (Melody Maker, 2 September 1978)

Angus MacKinnon & Charles Shaar Murray: RAR, It's Number One, It's Top of the Agitpops (New Musical Express, 24 March 1979)

Chris Brazier: Terrace Culture, Football and Rock (Melody Maker, 22 April 1978)

Chris Brazier: Siouxsie: A Confrontation (Melody Maker, 17 June 1978)

Dave McCullough & Garry Bushell: The Clash interview (Sounds, 14 July 1979)

Elly De Waard: Punk: wij zijn geen beesten en dat zijn wij ook nooit geweest (Vrij Nederland, 24 december 1977)

Garry Bushell: The Punk Years (Sounds Colour Magazine, 17 May 1986)

Ian Birch: Rough Trade, the Humane Sell (Melody Maker, 10 February 1979)

Ian Penman: Beat, Activity and Conversation (New Musical Express, 10 February 1979)

Jacky Huys: Is er leven na punk? (WeekendPlus Showkrant, 24 november 1979)

John Orme: Crisis? This Crisis! Crisis Time for the Record Business (Melody Maker, 10 June 1979)

Lena Andersson & Britt Ågren: Dom kallar oss punkare (Dagens Nyheter, 21, 28 April and 5 May 1979)

Mary Harron: Dialectics Meet Disco (Melody Maker, 26 May 1979)

Maryse Van Hee: Help, mijn kind is een punker (Panorama / Ons Land, 23 juli 1982)

Michael Watts: The Rise & Fall of Malcolm McLaren (Melody Maker, 16, 23 and 30 June 1979)

Mike Nicholls: JR Wants You For A Sunbeam (Record Mirror, 28 July 1979)

Mimo: Punk, pubers op de protesttoer (1977)

Neil Spencer: Sid Vicious, May 10 1957 - February 2 1979 (New Musical Express, 10 February 1979)

Paul Morley & Adrian Thrills: Independent Discs (New Musical Express, 1 September 1979)

Paul Morley: Oh Lucky Man! John Peel, this is your life (New Musical Express, 18 August 1978)

Peter de Koninck & Max Borka: Ooit lag er zeep in Cinderella's lavabo (Uitkrant, 25 oktober 1985)

Simon Frith: Afterpunk, The Different Drummer (Melody Maker, 31 March 1979)

Simon Kinnersley: Strummer Speaks: We Have Worked Ourselves Into A Corner (Melody Maker, 11 March 1978)

Steve Clarke: Master-minding the Militant Roadshow (New Musical Express, 31 March 1979)

Tijdschrift voor Diplomatie: Punk, rechtse reactie op werkloosheid (Maart 1978)

Tom Forester: The Return of the Mods (New Society, 24 May 1979)